ROAD TO BREXIT

Democracy in Action

W. A. Hoodless

First published 2017
Create Space Independent Publishing

ISBN-10: 1542397103
ISBN-13: 978-1542397100

Cover picture: **Big Ben by W A Hoodless**

DEDICATION

United Kingdom of Great Britain and Northern Ireland

Other books by the same author

Hengistbury Head, The Whole Story
(Poole Historical Trust 2005)

Air Raid. A Diary and Stories from the Essex Blitz
(History Press 2008)

Old Town Halls of Christchurch
(Natula Publications 2009)

Christchurch Curiosities
(History Press 2010)

Bournemouth Curiosities
(History Press 2012)

CONTENTS

	Acknowledgements	1
1	The Crux	3
2	Main Players	9
3	Perceived Need	13
4	Vote Remain Case	19
5	Force of History	37
6	Vote Leave Case	47
7	Campaign	61
8	Vote	69
9	Day After Review	81
10	Looking Ahead	105
11	Reflection	125
12	Index	129

ACKNOWLEDGMENTS

The many news reporters, politicians and friends on both sides of the debate

1 The Crux

"No one pretends that democracy is perfect or all-wise. Indeed it has been said that democracy is the worst form of Government except for all those other forms that have been tried from time to time ...."

Sir Winston Churchill

The purpose of this book is to write with balance about the UK Referendum of 23 June 2016 up to and including the following day, 24 June 2016. So committed were the two sides to their opinions, the Leave result meant no let-up in the emotional fight: Leavers were generally jubilant whilst Remainers were extremely sad and many of them very angry.

The crux of the campaign and vote was the strongly-held opposing attitudes and opinions of the two sides: Remainers were pro-EU saying that problems were either non-existent or could be solved whilst Leavers were anti-EU saying the problems were so serious that the UK should reclaim its independence. Was it a case of Brexit being a leap in the dark that would lead to economic catastrophe? Or, was the far greater risk that of staying with a dysfunctional EU with its anti-democratic nature and no chance to challenge its bad policies?

The list below gives the 28 countries of the EU as existing with the 19 members of the Eurozone marked by asterisks.

Austria *	*Germany* *	*Poland*
Belgium *	*Greece* *	*Portugal* *
Bulgaria	*Hungary*	*Romania*
Croatia	*Ireland* *	*Slovakia* *
Cyprus *	*Italy* *	*Slovenia* *
Czech Republic	*Latvia* *	*Spain* *
Denmark	*Lithuania* *	*Sweden*
Estonia *	*Luxembourg* *	*United Kingdom*
Finland *	*Malta* *	
France *	*Netherlands* *	

In one of the most significant UK votes ever cast, the British nation decided on a high turnout of 72% to leave the European Union by a margin of 3.8%, i.e. Leave 51.9%, Remain 48.1%. The exit by Britain is commonly termed Brexit. It happened despite the Conservative Government, the Liberal Democrats and the Labour Party all recommending the people to vote Remain. The words Vote Leave in this book generally refer to the exit movement as a whole rather than the officially approved group of that name.

The two most important people in the whole affair are probably Prime Minister David Cameron and UKIP leader Nigel Farage. It was the PM, statesmanlike politically skilled and generally lucky, who called the Referendum and Farage, controversial a brilliant speaker and tenacious, who did more over many years than anyone else to force the pace and make it necessary.

The main case put forward to Remain was the economic disaster to be expected after a Leave vote. The slogan was Stronger in Europe. Here are some claims listed at the start of the Government pamphlet urging Remain:

The UK has secured a special status in a reformed EU because we will not join the euro; we will keep our own border controls; the UK will not be part of further European integration; there will be tough new restrictions on access to our welfare system for new EU migrants; we have a commitment to reducing EU red tape; to

4

Remain would be in the best interests of people in the UK; this leaflet shows some choices if there is a vote to Leave.

The main case to Leave was the idea of taking back control of the country from the unelected bureaucrats in Brussels. One main slogan was UKIP Believes in Britain.

We should Vote Leave on 23 June because the PM's deal leaves the EU in charge of the same things after his negotiation as before; it is not legally binding and could be torn up by the EU the day after the referendum; we will keep sending £350 million every week to EU; immigration will continue out of control putting public services like the NHS under strain; the European Court will be in charge of our borders, immigration and asylum; by voting Leave we can take back control and spend our money on our priorities.

During the heavily publicized campaign period, there was no doubt about the pressures from the two sides as to how the public should vote.

The book sets the scene with the main players followed by the perceived need for the Referendum, the case for Remain and the force of history. By the time the case for Leave is reached, it is obvious that here was a most heated and at times, dark debate. After a description of the campaign and the Vote, some of the main comments, hopes and fears of people are reviewed on the Day After, 24 June 2016. Finally, there is a look to the future from that date and some reflection about the significance of Brexit.

Virtually no comments or events have been taken into account since the Day After, thus allowing a comparison between the Referendum and its immediate outcome on the one hand and the reader's knowledge of the subsequent events on the other. The Vote was Thursday 23 June 2016 and its result known the next day. For the chapters about the Vote and the following day therefore, I have only looked at live media up to 24 June and newspapers up to 25 June.

The success of the Leave side showed a big divide in the country between the Remainers including the Establishment, politicians, celebrities, the very well-off, the banks and the City, and the Leavers including those generally less well-off who felt excluded from the benefits of the EU.

The UK Referendum 2016 is an excellent example of how democracy can actually work and how powerful it can be. Indeed, one has to assume that Churchill was being serious in the quote above but not in the one which follows:

"The best argument against democracy is a five-minute conversation with the average voter!"

I have tried to avoid bias, covering events and comments only; my standpoint is that of an observer who has never been actively involved with politics. Although I have written several historical books, none has had such a strong political element as applies here.

It may also be helpful for me to explain the number of questions in the text. Throughout the campaign and its aftermath, there were judgements to be made on the issue of "Why?" Often there is a likely answer I can suggest with an element of confidence. However, there are other cases with plausible opposing responses. Since these are usually such subjective questions, I felt it better to raise them for the reader rather than give my own view. The next paragraph is one example: "Why organise a referendum when we already have a good democracy of elected representatives?"

A key question for the reader may be to ask if a referendum is appropriate to take extremely important national decisions or whether the historic method of electing governments based on party manifestos is always adequate. One might say that a General Election will not always be effective for a matter of such overarching importance, not least because of the large and growing remoteness of the main parties at Westminster. But, perhaps the reader's answer will depend on whether he or she supports the outcome of the Referendum.

The necessary research included the internet. Sometimes, it was possible to verify or check what are believed to be the facts. However, since this could not always be done, the reader should generally regard information as only having the status of being reported. Any errors that remain must be my own responsibility. Where material is still in copyright and it has been possible to establish that, I have the permission of the owners to reproduce it. I would however apologise for any accidental offence that may have been caused in cases where I have been unable to trace the owner.

Time to dive into the fray with the key players involved.

2   Main Players

"What we wish we readily believe, and what we ourselves think, we imagine others think also."

Julius Caesar

Who were the key figures who wanted to stay in the EU or wanted to leave it?

The Referendum was very different from a General Election because it really was one person one vote, with the result containing no inbuilt bias caused by the size and party composition of constituencies. The 52% Leave Vote simply meant that 52% had decided to Vote Leave. It was a major achievement for the Leavers with their relative lack of support from pollsters, celebrities, politicians, experts and big business.

Registered electorate

With every voter having an equal chance, the biggest players were indeed the British people, as influenced or otherwise by the pundits. The enormous organisations with their vested interests had much less clout. A referendum will take away power from elected representatives and return it to the citizens for that single issue, in this case, demonstrating a huge gulf between the largely pro-EU MPs and their constituents. Although there were plenty of advisors, the deciders were the voters.

Leavers

Whilst a number of politicians changed sides as the Referendum approached, it is probably unhelpful to speculate just why that happened. The most high-profile Leavers included:

Boris Johnson, MP, ex-Mayor of London
Michael Gove, Secretary of State for Justice
Andrea Leadsom, Minister of State for Energy
Nigel Farage, Leader of UK Independence Party
Gisela Stuart, Chair of Vote Leave and MP
James Dyson known for his inventions
Lord Anthony Bamford known for his JCBs
Tim Martin, founder of Wetherspoons.

Remainers

Those main players wanting to stay in the EU were much greater in numbers and, in most matters, influence including:

At least 70% of MPs
The banks and big companies like Ford
David Cameron, Prime Minister
George Osborne, Chancellor of the Exchequer
Jeremy Corbyn, Leader of the Labour Opposition
Amber Rudd, Secretary of State for Energy and Climate Change
Nicola Sturgeon, Leader of the Scottish Nationalists
Barack Obama, President of USA
Other members of the EU
Most celebrities

Other parties

On 13 April 2016, the Electoral Commission identified the two lead campaigners for the EU Referendum – designating 'The In Campaign Ltd.' Britain Stronger in Europe to be the lead campaigner for "Remain", and 'Vote Leave Ltd' for "Leave". There were however other bodies making the Leave case such as: UKIP, Leave.EU, the Bow Group, Global Britain, the Campaign Against Euro-federalism, Grassroots Out. The Remain Side also had the Liberal Democrats, the Greens and One Europe (Remain Great Remain In). However, TV and newspapers were all-important in conveying the arguments.

As always, the Queen stayed well above the highly emotional fray. Yet the Queen did suggest, four days before the Scottish Referendum for Independence of 18 September 2014 that voters should think very carefully about the future. Independence for Scotland was rejected. For the EU Referendum, the Daily Telegraph reported two days before the Vote that: The Queen has been canvassing opinion on the EU debate by asking dinner companions: "Give me three good reasons why Britain should be part of Europe".

Although it may be debateable by a few, most agree that the BBC has always been pro-Europe, a preference considered by many Leavers to be very evident during the reporting of events leading up to the Vote. But in my view anyway, attempts were made to be impartial with equal numbers from the two camps being invited to studio discussions.

The robust British Press provided very full coverage throughout the campaign from both points of view. Many were surprised to see that the Daily Mail was supporting Leave whilst the Mail on Sunday supported Remain, even referring to the other side as the "Leave mob". The Daily Express and Sun were for Leave whilst the Guardian, Financial Times and Mirror were for Remain.

Conduct of debate (Could this be a main player?)

Some TV debates suffered from people shouting at the same time, so making it hard for viewers to grasp the arguments.

Since passions ran high, it is unsurprising that there were many personal attacks including "blue on blue" within the Tory ranks. In one key TV debate, Johnson (Conservative), Stuart (Labour) and Leadsom (Conservative) were Leavers and Sturgeon (Scottish Nationalist), Rudd (Conservative) and Eagle (Labour) were Remainers. It included particularly strong attacks by the Remain Side described by one viewer afterwards as the Three Rottweilers. The voting public were probably not impressed.

Whilst the Remain Side focussed on the economic argument and dire consequences in the event of Brexit, the Leave Side felt that democracy, which enables the control of immigration, was more important. At least, these main thrusts became clear through the media.

Did the emotional conduct of the debate influence the outcome such that the conduct itself became a main player? Perhaps the weight of official support for Remain inadvertently gave the impression that voters were being "talked down to" and told how they should vote. Were voters tempted to decide based on their liking or otherwise for personalities and their methods? On balance, it is possible but unsafe to conclude the conduct swung the result one way or the other.

I should now like to turn to the origin of Brexit, the forces and the circumstances which impelled the Prime Minister to call the Referendum.

3   Perceived Need

"If you do not change direction, you may end up where you are heading."

Lao Tzu

Why have a referendum? A large part of the country is perfectly happy with Britain's membership of the European Union. Who is to say that UK regulations would be any better than EU ones? In a globalised world, should Europe not stand as a single powerful unit? At least 70% of MPs, who are, after all, in the best position to judge the matter, are EU supporters. The validity of all of these arguments for taking no action, was hotly disputed.

There has been an increasingly strong movement to leave the EU because of uncontrolled immigration putting public services, particularly housing, schools and the NHS, under unbearable strain. Moreover, human rights legislation, as policed by the EU, has produced a steady stream of unpopular court decisions which always seem to protect the miscreant at the expense of the victim. The failure to implement the 2010 Conservative manifesto pledge, to replace the EU human rights legislation by a new British Bill of Rights, has been much resented. Not least, the euro has been a disaster. In contrast, EU supporters said that the large number of immigrant workers has boosted the economy.

Since it can already be seen that there is a danger of promoting the views of one side or the other, I must say again that is not the purpose of the book. When an opinion is expressed in these pages, it is descriptive only, i.e. simply an iteration of what someone has said and not the author's opinion. Hence, the chapter heading is Perceived Need and not Need.

PERCEIVED NEED EXAMPLES

Democracy and Sovereignty

There has been a transfer of power from member nations to a kind of European super-state which has no meaningful democratic process. There is no way people can hold the EU to account through the ballot box. The EU Parliament is partly in Strasbourg and partly, for more of the year, in Brussels. Indeed, can one imagine any democratic government successfully persuading voters to relocate the parliament from one city to another city for four days every month?

It is unacceptable that so many powers have been transferred from Britain as a sovereign state to the EU. Since the latter is dysfunctional, poorly performing and corrupt, it is only right to give British voters a chance to Vote Leave. It is not acceptable that most of UK legislation is now initiated in the anti-democratic EU.

Immigration

Pressure, from unlimited EU immigration, has meant a disaster for public services. Housing, schools and hospitals cannot cope at present nor can the Government plan for the future without any proper idea of numbers. The incompetent EU has also failed to limit non-EU economic migrants from Africa and the Middle East.

Economy

Low wages accepted by immigrants, particularly from Eastern Europe, depress wages for British people and keep unemployment too high amongst the native population. The one-size-fits-all euro has caused terrific distress and unemployment in countries like Greece which desperately need their own currency and their own exchange rate. The euro has been maintained for political reasons to encourage unity but its effect has been the opposite. By leaving the EU, the UK would avoid future risk of damage by the euro.

Corruption

Every year for 20 years, public money has disappeared from the EU in ways that have not been traced. According to the "Organised Crime and Corruption: Cost of Non-Europe Report," corruption costs the EU 218 – 282 billion euros annually. This comment is an extract from a March 2016 study under the European Parliamentary Research Service Blog.

No-one has been found to be responsible and the annual accounts have not been signed off as satisfactory by auditors. The EU appears to make no progress in resolving this scandal. It is particularly unsatisfactory for the UK and Germany who subsidise the rest of the EU.

Bureaucracy and costs

The high-spending tendency of the EU appears to have no bounds. The massive, expensive, unnecessary transfer of the European Parliament from Brussels to Strasbourg and back has already been mentioned. MEPs are lavishly overpaid. Whilst member nations go through painful austerity programmes, EU costs spiral ever upwards. Much of the legislation is anti-competitive and should be scrapped.

Conservative Party politics

As explained in the Force of History chapter, Europe has been a very divisive issue for the Party having a real impact on its ability to win elections. Since the EU is what may be termed Modern Socialist, it is much less divisive for the Labour Party. Hence, the PM had a key reason for calling the Referendum: to try and secure an acceptable outcome for his Party, so settling the European Question and bringing together the Conservatives for the future. A united Tory Party would indeed be a good prize to secure.

Human rights

Whatever may be the merits and theory of human rights legislation, it really does not work in practice. The Universal Declaration of Human Rights by the UN in 1948 may have been an attempt to ban forever the barbarities which happen in war. But as operated by the EU, more rights are given to the miscreants than their victims. Many consider that the whole concept of an outlaw, whereby a criminal is denied normal rights, has been lost. For example, why should an illegal immigrant who commits murder have any ability to avoid deportation to his own country, merely because he claims a right to family life in UK or that his home country is unsafe?

Despite many such cases which are dramatically described by the newspapers week in week out, there seems to be no will for reform. Meanwhile, the Conservative Manifesto pledge to replace the legislation with a Bill of Rights has yet to be honoured.

RESPONSES TO PERCEIVED NEEDS, AND REACTIONS

The most common response has been that although there are some problems with the nature and structure of the EU, these can be resolved by working with other member nations in order to make improvements. The reaction to or difficulty with that response, is that there are many examples where UK representations have failed to achieve agreement and improvement.

Another response is that the EU problems can always be settled and in any case, are much less important than keeping the peace in Europe. The answer to that approach is to say that the EU has done nothing to keep the peace because that has been achieved by NATO. If anything, the harsh austerity requirements, imposed on the poorer countries by the EU, have caused a huge amount of unnecessary friction.

Since the biggest single feature of perceived need is perhaps the "open borders problem" causing uncontrolled immigration, the complete failure of the Government to tackle it has proved highly unpopular. With a promise to reduce net immigration to less than 100,000 p.a. first made by the Conservatives for the 2010 General Election and repeated for the 2015 one, many felt disenfranchised to see it climbing to over 300,000 by 2015. The Remain Side's response to this main issue has proved tactless and unacceptable, i.e. that immigration is good for the country and need not be limited. Nor did it help anyone when the Remainers tried to label the Leavers as racist.

So what exactly were the Remainers saying in order to rebut the perceived need for a referendum and the case for Leave? Their arguments are next.

4   Vote Remain Case

"The European Union Treaty… within a few years will lead to the creation of what the founding fathers of modern Europe dreamed of after the war, the United States of Europe."

Helmut Kohl

INTRODUCTION

Although democracy can deliver the unexpected, most prefer it to the only alternative which is some form of dictatorship. There may be a case for a Benign Dictatorship or to say that sovereignty does not exist because no country can control everything affecting it. Perhaps a more common opinion is to say a nation is like a ship sailing through changing sea conditions. Although the captain cannot change those conditions, he should not give away control of the ship to anyone outside it.

Part of the difficulty for the voter was understanding the nature of the EU. What is it exactly? Some Leavers have been known to refer to the Brussels Dictatorship whilst some Remainers see the EU as a beneficial protector of all within its borders. Does the truth lie somewhere in between? Inevitably, the debate has brought out a high level of personal prejudice with claims ranging from nobility of purpose to a dastardly and incompetent gravy train. Would voters see the EU as a force for peace? Are Remainers trying to give away control of the ship?

The Uncertainty Issue, described at the start of the later chapter dealing with the Vote Leave Case, is also relevant for this one, covering as it does inadequately supported opinions and responses. Moreover, perhaps in part because Leavers and Remainers were quite evenly matched, tempers were increasingly lost. A common criticism was that those losing the argument resorted to personal attacks. Suffice it to say that voters were not helped by such attacks made by both sides.

There has also been some confusion caused by the overlap of arguments. For example, any reference to the Single Market can often bring in other issues like free movement or continued UK contributions to the EU. I must ask the reader to indulge the element of repetition in these pages in the hope of a better overall understanding. However, before considering the Remainers' claims and the responses, let us look at the Official Recommendation.

OFFICIAL RECOMMENDATION

A very strong push was made by the powers-that-be to Vote Remain, an impetus which went well beyond the stereotype of the London Metropolitan Elite, i.e. the so-called arrogant and hypocritical liberal intelligentsia many of whom seemed to live in Notting Hill and were criticised for so doing. Whilst certain people seemed to fit this description, they were not numerous enough to swing the Vote.

A key example of the Official Recommendation was the Government's pamphlet sent to all 27 million households in the country. One illustration was captioned that the UK was not part of the European border-free zone, adding that we control our own borders. It may be that the pamphlet was counter-productive because it was commonly known that the manifesto pledge, to restrict net immigration to no more than 100,000 p.a., had totally failed. Costing £9.3 million, the highly controversial 14 page booklet was announced in April 2016 and fully distributed by May. Boris Johnson described it as biased, hysterical and warning unnecessarily of risks. He thought it unhelpful and that any such Government advice should give <u>both</u> sides of the debate.

Apart from the recommendation to Vote Remain from the existing majority Conservative Government, the Labour Party also had the same policy. Although many felt that the historically Eurosceptic leader, Jeremy Corbyn, ran a lacklustre campaign, he nonetheless advised to vote for the Remain Side. The Liberal Democrats and Greens were also for Remain. It was reported that 10 Downing Street had persuaded many captains of industry to issue supporting statements for the Official Recommendation to Remain, and so it transpired. The pro-EU BBC made strenuous, though not fully successful, efforts to be impartial during the campaign. The banks and Bank of England favoured Remain. In this era of celebrity worship, there were also many highly-publicised (though not particularly thought-provoking) statements from celebrity Remainers.

It is a moot point whether the huge majority for Remain, amongst the powers-that-be, enhanced the Remain Vote. Perhaps the opposite is true because many voters became tired of the pressure from the Remainers and their so-called experts.

As the Referendum date approached, it dominated the news, well and truly capturing the imagination and emotions of the country. Just then, there was a brutal killing, felt by many to be Referendum-related.

MURDER OF JO COX, MP

This tragic event took place at the height of the campaign leading to terrific publicity. Since it could have been influential on the voting, it is included here just before the Remainers' Claims.

On 16 June 2016, Jo Cox (41), Labour MP for Batley and Spen, was shot and stabbed multiple times when about to attend a constituency meeting in Birstall, West Yorkshire. Reportedly, a doctor pronounced her dead at the scene and suspect Tommy Mair (52) was arrested by police. Police were reported to be investigating a claim that the suspect shouted "Britain first," a possible reference to a small far-right political party. That party later denied any involvement. When asked his name in court on 18 June, Mair said "Death to traitors, freedom for Britain."

The popular MP had won the seat for Labour in 2015 with an increased majority and was widely recognised as a dedicated politician. Tommy Mair, who was duly charged with murder, had a history of mental illness and also connection with far-right parties. Her widower, Brendan Cox issued a statement urging people to "fight against the hatred that killed her" and asked for donations to three of her favourite charities. Such was the publicity and the public reaction that £1 million had been donated by 20 June. Oxfam released an album, Glastonbury Festival began with a tribute and President Obama phoned Brendan Cox with his condolences. Parliament was recalled on 20 June to enable MPs to pay tribute to Jo Cox. The news was dominated by the murder for a week before the Referendum. It was a major story and one which could not have helped the Leave Side.

At a memorial service in Trafalgar Square held on 22 June, Brendan was speaking to the crowds, as relayed live to a huge throng in Market Place, Batley:

"Jo's killing was political, it was an act of terror designed to advance an agenda of hatred towards others. What a beautiful irony it is that an act designed to advance hatred has instead generated such an outpouring of love. Jo lived for her beliefs, and on Thursday she died for them, and for the rest of our lives we will fight for them in her name."

The New Yorker commented:

"Many in Market Place wept openly as those words were spoken, and it was difficult to imagine anyone who could have listened to that speech, and then voted to leave the European Union."

We shall probably never know what impact this tragedy had on the voting public. Without making direct claims, the media gave the impression that the alleged murderer was a very right wing member of the Brexit camp. But there seems to be no evidence to suggest that the media had any political agenda. If, as a result of the murder, many floaters were persuaded to Vote Remain that would be unfortunate because it seems that it was a case of mental illness and thus not relevant to the Referendum.

However, the alleged killer is reportedly to be put on trial as a terrorist in November 2016. Certainly, it is fair to say that Leavers were just as shocked as Remainers. After voting day, the media profile of the murder appeared to be much reduced.

REMAINERS' CLAIMS

In the same way as for Leavers' claims later in the book, responses are given for each of these Remainers' claims.

The EU has unified Europe, so preventing another world war

Europe was very sick and very tired after the massive killing of two world wars between 1914 and 1945: just 31 years, many millions killed and for what? This indeed is the origin of the European Project. Such wars must not be allowed to recur. By bringing the nations together for the first time, we should never again have to endure the horrors of the past. The ongoing peace is testament to the success of the EU and must not be put at risk by the UK Voting Leave. To build on this success, there is to be a new European Army controlled from Brussels.

Response: The causes of World War I lay in the nineteenth century web of alliances and the ambitions of the Kaiser. This no longer applies. As for World War II, that arose from a growing international fascist movement cleverly exploited by Hitler who demonised the Jews and the unfair Versailles Treaty. Again, despite any nobility of purpose in the Treaty of Rome, the causes of World War II no longer apply. In fact, since the real post-1945 threat has been the Cold War, as deterred by NATO and NATO alone, the EU has not done anything significant to prevent war. It was very much a standoff between the US-led NATO and Russia, going right back to the time of the Cuban Missile Crisis and the days of Kennedy and Khrushchev. The idea of a new European Army, having British troops under foreign control, is merely another instance of unacceptable loss of sovereignty. A vote in the Daily Express had 93% saying the EU Army was a terrible idea and only 7% saying yes, it would make us more secure.

Thus, although the European Project may have arisen from a noble cause, there is now a huge irony: the misguided EU policies on the euro and immigration have created great tension and resentment amongst member nations. This increase in nationalism could lead to conflict after a future collapse of the EU.

The Government's renegotiation with the EU justifies Vote Remain

When the PM made a promise to the UK in January 2013 that there would be an In/Out Referendum, he said that he would renegotiate the UK's terms of membership and then recommend accordingly. In February 2016, his recommendation to Remain was clear because of the improved terms in the Cameron Deal. In brief, these were:

1. Britain to be excluded from ever-closer political integration in EU.
2. Britain to be able to apply to EU for a seven year consent to limit payment of in-work benefits to new EU migrants, as phased over four years. The EU first to be satisfied that EU migration was putting excessive pressure on public services, and consent for this emergency brake to lapse after the seven

years. The benefits, tax credits, to be increased in phases for each migrant from zero to full over four years.

3. When an existing EU migrant has children still living abroad, child benefits to be reduced in phases from 2020, i.e. "to index such benefits to the conditions of the Member State where the child resides." This phrase means there would be a link to the cost of living in the Member State and payments would be made at local rates. For new arrivals, the rules would apply at once.

4. Britain, as a non-member of the Eurozone, not to be liable to help fund euro bailouts, and also, to be able to challenge any proposed regulation that would discriminate against the UK. The latter would operate by requiring an urgent discussion in the 28 member European Council. In addition, all must comply with a single financial rulebook to ensure a level playing field.

Response: This understanding with the EU is a watered-down version of the original very limited demands by the PM. It does nothing to stop free movement of labour or to reform farm payments or to repatriate employment law or to change the working hours' directive. This last means that doctors' hours would continue to be set by Brussels. Despite the Conservative manifesto commitment that EU migrants would not even be considered for social housing for at least four years after arrival in an area, this change was not even included in the PM's negotiations. Item 1 above does not deal with the mass of existing red tape and regulations which would continue in force. Item 2 depends on an EU approval, is very limited and is only temporary. Item 3 permits child benefits to continue to be sent to home countries. The rulebook provision in Item 4 does not protect the City from future harmful EU regulation such as the Tobin tax. All in all, the renegotiation provides little improvement for the UK and does not justify a Remain Vote. Even if it did, there is a lot of doubt about whether the renegotiation is legally binding, subject as it is to the EU courts and EU Parliament.

UK will keep its own border controls

Since the UK is not part of the EU border-free zone known as the Schengen Agreement (which permits passport free movement over most of EU), we can check all incomers including EU nationals. The Cameron Deal means that the benefits system here is less attractive to migrants and in any case, a country like Norway (which is a Schengen country though not in the EU) has to accept free movement in order to have access to the Single Market.

Response: All this is academic. The important point is that all EU citizens have the right to live and work in the UK as long as we stay in the EU. Border checks do not stop that and the sheer attractiveness of the UK to economic migrants is why immigration from the EU is excessive and should be controlled. For example, National Insurance statistics show that 630,000 EU nationals migrated to UK in 2015. As for the Single Market, access would continue in the event of Brexit and probably on the same terms because the EU exports to the UK are more than the UK exports to the EU, i.e. if tariffs were raised, they would hurt the EU the most. Since the recession-hit EU economy is in a much worse state than that of the euro-free UK, there would be no post-Brexit attempt to block trade with the UK.

UK will not join the Eurozone

Although it is widely accepted that the euro has been a problem for some countries in the EU, that is not a risk to the UK because of the Cameron Deal. It means that the exchange rate for the pound can fluctuate as may be needed and the country can benefit accordingly.

Response: Assuming the Deal would apply without being stopped by the EU courts or EU Parliament, it simply means continued exemption from one of the big disadvantages of the EU rules. However, as the second biggest net contributor to the cost of running the EU, the UK would still be saddled with paying for the failed euro policy one way or another. For example, the austerity package forced on Greece by the EU is not only part of the cause for their 50% youth unemployment, but also means endless bailouts by other members and issues of debt relief. It needs an act of faith to accept the UK would not wind up paying for bailouts etc. under the Deal. The exemption may thus not be strong enough to resist the continuing core EU policy of extending the Eurozone to all members. If we Vote Remain, is not the ever-increasing cost of the EU the real leap in the dark for the UK?

There will be tough new restrictions on welfare for new EU migrants

New EU migrants will not have full access to certain benefits for four years. Moreover, the Government will have greater powers to take action against abuse of the immigration system, e.g. sham marriages.

Response: This so-called emergency brake, on in-work benefits such as tax credits, would have to be approved in advance by the EU and would expire anyway after seven years. Phasing it in would reduce its effectiveness such that the UK would still be just as strong a draw to migrants from poorer countries where the average wage is a small fraction of that in the UK. More importantly, the migrants want highly paid (relative to their home country) UK jobs not benefits, as shown by the very low figure of 84,000 EU migrant families claiming tax credits in 2014. As for sham marriages, there are already some measures to counteract this abuse.

Workers' rights have been safeguarded by the EU

A major benefit of the EU is the protection of workers' rights. Without this advantage, many hard working families would be at the mercy of government cuts and the threatened bonfire of the regulations.

Response: Since the UK has a proud history of spearheading the development of workers' rights, it requires no lessons on the subject from the EU. Besides, it is better for such things to be decided by the democratic government of the country rather than by unelected officials who are not accountable to the voters.

UK will not be part of further political integration

As one of the terms of the Cameron Deal, this assurance means we will not be part of the progressive political union of the EU into a super-state with ever more powers transferred from individual members.

Response: This is really a political aspiration but without legal force. It does not come close to the UK winning back control of its own affairs via Brexit and no existing EU laws would be changed for the UK. In addition, the words used, ever closer union, do not in law imply a move to a federal EU so that a UK exemption will not change her legal relationship with the EU. Observation shows that ever closer union in the EU is a mission that is being achieved by the endless stream of laws sent from Brussels to member nations. In short, only Brexit would deliver no further political integration.

There is a commitment to reduce EU red tape

The commitment applies to all red tape across the board and means there will be better regulation.

Response: The reality is that nothing has changed with this failed aspiration. In fact, this EU commitment is now over ten years old and there is no sign of any red tape reduction. There are still excessive and unnecessary administration costs borne by both businesses and public bodies.

Britain is safer in the EU

The police can use intelligence from the other 27 countries in the EU and have access to fingerprint and DNA information. This sort of cooperation makes it easier to keep criminals and terrorists out of UK whilst the European Arrest Warrant (EAW) has brought many to justice. All this could be lost in the event of Vote Leave.

Response: It will still be in the interests of all to cooperate fully against criminals and terrorists. The EU will not be interested in reducing any country's security. Vote Leave would however enable the return of the traditional blue British passport that would allow effective border checks for incomers to UK. Even the EAW has been applied in a controversial way so allowing the British Press to point to injustices.

The Referendum was unnecessary and should never have been called

It always was a high risk strategy to call the Referendum and perhaps have to lose access to the highly beneficial EU Single Market.

It is better by far to play one's part within the EU than to try to act independently in a globalised world. For example, Sinn Fein took the view all along that the PM had made a major mistake in calling the Referendum which appeals to Little Englanders. Martin McGuinness, Deputy First Minister of Northern Ireland, actually forecast that David Cameron was sleepwalking to a Brexit vote. The UK is not able to survive effectively without having the benefits of EU membership.

Response: On the contrary, it was right and inevitable to obtain the people's opinion on an ever-expanding and increasingly controlling EU because sovereignty has always been very important. With even more powers being planned for transfer to the EU from member states, the UK has to be given the choice. If many small countries can manage on their own in the world, the UK, shown by the IMF in 2016 as the world's fifth biggest economy and contributing 17% to EU GDP, can do the same. The UK is "good enough" and up to the task.

Over three million jobs are linked to exports to EU

Such jobs would obviously be at risk from Brexit. The free trade area of 500 million population is indispensable to the UK. It is folly to lose access to this hugely beneficial Single Market.

Response: It is also the case that over five million EU jobs are linked to trade with the UK. Therefore, we can be sure that EU businesses will do all they can to ensure continued favourable access to the UK market. The EU would have to abide by the normal requirement of political decisions following trade pressures, as in the common saying "trade trumps politics". Post-Brexit negotiations would not result in any significant trade barriers or impact on jobs. Not least, Brexit would enable the UK to build trading deals with the wide world beyond the EU. Since well over 90% of the world's population is outside the EU, that is a great opportunity. Finally, exchange rate changes are much more important to trading volumes than moving from the Single Market to the alternative, i.e. World Trade Organisation rules.

The EU has made travel to Europe easier and cheaper

Lower cost flights have been made possible within the EU and from next year mobile phone roaming charges will no longer apply saving UK customers up to 38p per minute on calls. There is also free or cheap access to public healthcare. Such benefits would be at risk under Brexit.

Response: Here is another Project Fear implication, i.e. that travel would become much more expensive and difficult in the event of Brexit. Already, some 50 countries have visa-free travel to the EU and London is the most visited city for EU nationals. There would continue to be easy and economical travel from the UK because that is in the interests of both UK and EU. There would be little change.

Author's Note: A major and frequent difficulty of the voting public was deciding what to believe. Here is a common example of "yes it is; no it isn't". According to the Remain Side, Brexit brings a dire risk of losing valuable EU travel benefits whilst according to the Leave Side, that is all part of Project Fear. The huge missing element is a <u>factual</u> statement one way or the other. That was because no-one could prove a claim that was dependent on future negotiations; one simply had to take a view. Is it any wonder that, as will be seen in the chapter on the Vote, it was reported that about 9% to 10% of voters only reached their decision on polling day?

The UK would not get the benefit of the essential trade deals now being negotiated by the EU with Japan and the USA

As part of the EU, Britain would have the benefit of these deals. But in the event of Brexit, Britain would be without EU support and thus struggle to make her own trading arrangements. President Obama has said that the UK would have to be at the back of the queue after the EU, so causing delays lasting years.

Response: Although desirable, you do not <u>need</u> a trade deal to carry on trade; there is none at present with America yet there is enormous trade in progress. The truth is that since the EU is difficult to deal with owing to the protectionism of many member states, the UK would settle free trade matters more swiftly and efficiently alone. The result would be lower priced goods for the public. It simply must be better for the UK not to be prevented, by virtue of her EU membership, from arranging trade terms with the big developing economies of the world.

Vote Leave would mean a collapse of the pound and the stock market

The sheer uncertainty arising from leaving the EU would have a disastrous effect on business confidence. Once that happens, the pound would be greatly devalued and the stock market would crash. Making imports much more expensive and wiping many billions off company value is bad for the UK. Loss of our full access to the Single Market would make exports to EU harder. With higher prices in the shops and problems getting mortgages, living standards would be damaged.

Response: Although big business may see advantages to staying in the EU, such as being better able to cope with the endless regulations than their smaller competitors, any impact on the stock market would be temporary. Business would do what it always does: adapt to changing conditions to reach a fresh stability. If the pound devalued and stayed lower, that would be excellent for exporters and the economy in contrast to the disaster of the "one size fits all euro". Remember, the UK already exports more goods and services to the rest of the world than the EU and that business is growing. Certainly, any devaluation would increase pressure on the EU from EU businesses to maintain free trade with the UK.

Vote Leave would stop access to the Single Market unless the UK continued to pay for the EU and to permit unlimited immigration

How would the UK survive without its preferential access to the EU Single Market? It is vitally important for our exporters to be able to sell into that market on a free trade basis. Jobs are dependent on the UK export trade raising the prospect of a Leave Vote causing a big increase in unemployment. Being part of the EU makes the UK more attractive for investors in the UK. Despite the claims of the Leavers, the UK would be in the same position as Norway and Switzerland and have to pay in to the EU and still have immigration through free movement.

Response: Most UK exports already go to the rest of the world. With the EU being an economic basket case having very low economic growth, it is far better for the UK to expand its business outside the Single Market, i.e. with the 90% plus of the world population beyond the EU. Companies may have to adapt in the short term but the prospects for the country are much better if we Vote Leave and investment would continue. In any case, since the EU exports much more to the UK than the other way around, it is likely that free trade can continue without any tariff or free movement penalty being required. In short, UK exports to EU would continue but Brexit would enable a big increase in exports to the rest of the world. There is no reason why the Norwegian or Swiss model should apply to the UK.

If the UK left the EU, there would have to be big increases in taxation and cuts in public spending

The Chancellor of the Exchequer, George Osborne, said that there would have to be £30 billion taken out of the economy in the event of Brexit. As a result of uncertainty and other economic problems, it meant an emergency budget would be required with a mixture of public spending cuts and higher taxes.

Response: This is a good example of Project Fear from its chief proponent trying to frighten voters into supporting Remain. There is no credible justification for doing any such thing. Besides, any punishment budget would never get parliamentary approval.

Pensions would be reduced and there would be other bad financial impacts

Another of the Chancellor's arguments in favour of Remain was this one aimed at pensioners, as graphically shown in a Remain poster including a worried looking elderly lady with an empty purse. Brexit is so bad for the country that there could be no ongoing guarantee of protection for the elderly.

He also claimed that, in the event of Brexit, households would be £4,300 p.a. worse off on average by 2030.

With a 0.7% increase in mortgage rates, that would average another £920 p.a. cost increase for borrowers. The Treasury also forecast an average drop in house values of £20,000 would be attributable to Brexit.

Response: The image of a pensioner having an empty purse is simply disgraceful propaganda. It is unsupported by any proper calculations and is again trying to scare the people into voting Remain. Moreover, it takes no account of the legal protection of the triple lock, i.e. that state pensions will always rise by the highest of inflation, 2.5% and average earnings. Equally, the other figures are not properly evidenced and thus highly suspect.

Vote Leave would cause years of uncertainty and economic disruption

Investment and jobs would be lost whilst the UK unpicks the relationship with the EU and has to make new arrangements with other countries. It would be hard to arrange not least because while 44% of the UK exports go to the EU, only 8% of the EU exports go to the UK. The uncertainty could continue for 10 years and result in reduced access to the all-important Single Market.

Response: There would be a UK trade model negotiated with the EU, not one based on that of Norway or the current negotiations with Canada or any other country. The only reason that EU exports to UK are at 8% of the total is because the EU is much bigger than the UK. More relevant is that Britain is the biggest export market of all for the EU and is a huge benefit for the big manufacturers like the German company BMW. In particular, since the UK imports more from the EU than the other way around, higher tariffs would hurt the EU the most. It would thus be in the EU's interest to agree for the UK to continue its existing access without penalty.

Author's note: This is one of many disingenuous arguments advanced during the campaign by both sides. Taking the response merely as an example of the genre, it could be resisted by saying: "The EU as a whole is much better able to withstand a trade loss based on 8% of exports than could the UK withstand a loss based on 44% of exports, thereby giving the upper hand to the EU in any post-Brexit tariff negotiation." That said, the Leave Side never really stressed that the exchange rate is much more significant than the present access to the Single Market because the impact of WTO tariffs would be much less than say, a large drop in the value of the pound.

There are many benefits to the UK of EU membership

The EU promotes peace and economic security whilst allowing UK opt-outs such as keeping the pound and not being within the Schengen Area. No future powers can be transferred without a referendum. Only 1% of UK taxes goes to the EU thus being very good value for all the jobs and economic security received in return. There are opportunities for families to live, work or study in EU countries together with guarantees of many employment rights. The UK already holds the position of an independent, strong leading force in the world. Being in the EU magnifies its ability to get its way on the issues we care about. EU action helped prevent Iran from getting nuclear weapons and the EU leads the world on tackling climate change.

Response: Despite these "benefits" sounding good, the reality is different. Taking these claims mainly in order, the evidence for increased peace and security is missing; the opt-outs might be agreed as some damage limitation for the UK; future transfer of powers would be difficult to prevent; the 1% takes no account of the hardship and costs of the red tape; there would still be the chance of living/working in the EU; the EU actually diminishes UK influence by definition because a major degree of sovereignty has been surrendered; the world has not followed the lead of the EU in tackling climate change largely because of the unacceptably huge costs of its green policies. Finally, it is more accurate to say that the negotiations for Iran were undertaken by America, "as joined at the negotiating table by the world's major powers: the UK, France, Germany, Russia and China as well as the EU."

If the UK left the EU, it would not be able to survive on its own

The globalised world is difficult and threatening in a way that makes it essential for the UK to have the massive protection of the EU in order to survive. For at least 40 years, we have benefitted from all the help of the EU and could not manage without it. As they say in Brussels, individual nations are too small to cope and need to pool their sovereignty.

Response: Here we have yet another false claim as part of Project Fear. There would be no difficulty for the UK, as the world's fifth largest economy, in making her own arrangements in the same way as for the hundreds of years before joining the EU in 1973. In any case, with all its skills, the EU has not yet been able to make a trade agreement with America. Meanwhile, its poor economic performance continues, showing that it is not a good club for the UK.

The Leave campaign is run by ignorant, stupid, Little Englanders and racists who do not appreciate the many benefits of being part of the EU

Far too many want to return to the rather fictional model of 1950s England where all was well and everyone was happy. That is not the world of today, if indeed it ever really existed. We must embrace our future as part of the EU with all its benefits and ability to take decisions where necessary on our behalf. Like it or not, it is now a multi-cultural world of increasingly vibrant countries. We should be part of all that rather than trying to isolate ourselves as a small and inward-looking insignificant island offshore to mainland Europe. To quote actress Emma Thompson: "The UK is a little cloud-bolted rainy corner of sort-of Europe, a cake-filled, misery-laden grey old island."

Response: It is not stupid to want to control your own country through democracy nor is it racist to want to limit immigration to a level that can be managed. Nor is it inward-looking to plan more exports to the rest of the world. The other claims are without any supporting evidence. Farage was unimpressed by the quote, saying it was utterly defeatist and negative.

Vote Remain for a secure future as part of Europe

It would be a leap in the dark to try and leave the EU. There are many downsides, from failing to have the benefits of enough immigrants to fill the job vacancies, to severely damaging the economy. Trade works well at present and travel is simple by dint of the EU passport and the EU health card. All these 28 countries working together create a powerful bloc to deal with the world's problems from the economic ones to those affecting climate change. It should not be tampered with by Voting Leave.

Response: The case for unfettered immigration and economic benefit has not been made. Apart from the incomers overwhelming a very crowded country, what of all the British people who are unable to get a job or school place or GP appointment? What of the costs arising from the many different languages increasingly being spoken and the failure of foreign staff to have a good enough grasp of English to work safely in the NHS? The passport seems to have helped the ingress of terrorists whilst the climate change agenda continues to be ineffective and controversial. There is nothing of substance here to support the Remain Side.

CONTEXT OF THE DEBATE

It is very clear that the Remainers take the view that the future of the UK is best in ever closer integration with the EU. They do not see any particular benefit in maintaining sovereignty when there are believed to be net advantages to membership.

However, history, together with the resulting culture and sense of national identity, can have a rather tenacious power over us, more so than one might think. Hence, although it could have simply been included as one of the Main Players, I felt that separate treatment was essential. The next chapter looks at the sheer force of history.

5   Force of History

"Patriotism is supporting your country all the time and your government when it deserves it."

Mark Twain

EARLIER TIMES

What is the United Kingdom of Great Britain and Northern Ireland? Was the history of the country a major cause of strong opposition to the EU? In this brief chapter, it is only possible to provide an overview.

We live in an ice age currently having the benefit of a warm interglacial period, pending the next cold period. Since the interglacial began over 10,000 years ago, world civilisation has developed. The ice melt caused a rise in sea levels of some 400 feet, so creating the English Channel over 6,000 years ago and forming the island we now call Britain out of the mainland continent of Europe. By the time of Christ, the ice sheet, which originally extended down to the Thames, had retreated and the Britons had been able to develop arable and pasture farming.

Having civilised, or perhaps more accurately subjugated, the country over some 400 years, the Romans finally left in the early fifth century AD. There followed considerable settlement from mainland Europe by the Saxons, Jutes, Vikings and others up to the Norman Conquest of 1066 AD. We have indeed been both an island race and a mongrel race from the earliest of days.

Yet it is one which has developed feelings of great patriotism, as rather glorified for example in the remembrance of the Battle of Waterloo 1815. At that time, calls were made and heeded for the bridge under construction to be renamed from Strand Bridge to Waterloo Bridge in honour of the victory. When the nearby terminus opened in 1848, it was named Waterloo Station after the bridge. The railway travellers reach their terminus at Waterloo rather like Napoleon reached his terminus at Waterloo.

Even by the time of the Battle of Hastings in 1066, a cohesive and effective Saxon Government had been created. Indeed, William the Conqueror found a reasonably prosperous and contented people in the same way that Julius Caesar had discovered when he undertook his armed raid in 55 BC.

After the Norman Conquest, there were serious threats and upheavals caused by the need for Magna Carta in 1215, the rise and fall of royal dynasties, the Civil War in the seventeenth century and threats from the Spanish, French and Germans. But the Armada, Napoleon, the Kaiser and Hitler were all seen off by 1588, 1815, 1918 and 1945 respectively. Moreover, Nelson, virtually worshiped by many as a true national hero, has been credited with enabling Britain's mastery of the seas for a hundred years after Trafalgar in 1805.

In the nineteenth century, society fostered patriotism not least through the music halls and the schools. The international dispute leading to the Russo-Turkish War of 1877 to 1878 gave rise to Macdermott's War Song (1877) by G. W. Hunt. It was all about Jingoism which supported the policy of saving Constantinople from Russia. The chorus of this music hall hit included:

"We don't want to fight but by Jingo if we do, we've got the ships we've got the men and got the money too."

In the event, Disraeli secured the British preferred route to India by sending gunboats to the Turkish Straits, thus deterring Russia from deciding to take Constantinople from Turkey and closing the Straits to the British. Jingoism today is generally defined as going beyond an acceptable level of patriotism being somewhat too nationalistic and aggressive. But at the time, the fervour of the audience was real enough. Here is the end of the last verse before the last chorus:

"Let them be warned, Old England is brave Old England still,
We've proved our might, we've claimed our right, and ever, ever will,
Should we have to draw our sword, our way to victory we'll forge,
With the battle cry of Britons, Old England and St. George!"

With this song, the Great Macdermott boosted his singing career in the music hall, getting thunderous applause for it night after night at the London Pavilion. Even today, there is great public participation and applause for the patriotic songs of the Last Night of the Proms.

With the development of the unwritten British Constitution, the British Empire, world-leading inventiveness, heavy industry and literature, it is small wonder that most felt lucky to be in Great Britain, often described as the best country in the world. One proof of such a high level of patriotism lies in the enormous numbers of young men enlisting in 1914.

Thus, despite many disruptions since 1066, the British Isles remained broadly stable and politically intact, except of course for the grant of Irish independence in 1922. Part of the story has been the development of parliamentary democracy, generally held to be a gift from Great Britain to the world.

What then is the true historical context and timescale for the UK Referendum of 2016? The period since 1066 could be the most realistic. During that time of national development, the country's separation from the continent, by means of the English Channel, has been a major stabilising factor in what Churchill called our island story. Although he died in 1965, his ideas, like those of Shakespeare, remain much quoted. This following extract is from his crucial speech to the Cabinet in 1940. It was successful in killing the very idea of appeasing

Hitler, thus qualifying as one of the most important events of World War II:

"If this long island story of ours is to end at last, let it end only when each one of us lies choking in his own blood upon the ground."

A powerful speech indeed and one soaked in feelings of British independence.

The existence of the English Channel aided national defence, development of the common law and parliamentary democracy. Yet although an island, our history has always been closely linked to Europe. It certainly was in 1940.

In summary, although British people today are the result of immigration from many different places over the centuries, a clear sense of national identity and pride arose and continued to World War II and the 1950s. The social revolution, which began in the 1960s, has reduced that sense but has by no means eliminated it, even today.

Many voters understand the important way that Britain devised a democratic system based on the separation of powers but retaining the monarchy. By ensuring that the monarchy now plays a mainly ceremonial role, the country has removed a harmful source of conflict with Parliament. Thus the unwritten British Constitution ensures the valuable separation of the Three Powers of Government. Firstly, the Executive (Cabinet) identifies the need for, and initiates the implementation of, new laws. Secondly, the Legislature (Commons and Lords) carries into legal force those proposed laws deemed democratically acceptable. Thirdly, the fiercely independent Judiciary provides correct implementation of the law and is a check on any excesses planned by parties in Government. To these voters, the EU appears a very poor and undemocratic second best.

From the nineteenth century onwards, there have been two main political movements. To oversimplify, the Conservative Party has wanted to expand aspirations, business and profits whilst tending to keep the structure of society and minimise public spending. The Labour Party has wanted to transfer some wealth from the rich to the poor whilst supporting those in genuine need and increasing public spending. Although British Governments have alternated between Left and Right for around 100 years, they have had full sovereign authority and most agree that they always ruled in accord with their idea of the country's best interests.

Regular elections in the UK mean that voters can simply get rid of a poorly performing Government after four or five years – it is an effective democracy. In contrast, the EU does not operate in this way. Since the MEPs are unable to initiate legislation, they are reduced to voting on whatever is placed before them and its sheer quantity requires a very speedy process and limited scrutiny. UKIP apart, few rock the boat. It appears that all the real decisions are taken by the European Commission's appointed officers who are not accountable to any electorate. Whatever one's views about the merit of the EU, it is a totally different system of government from the one which has evolved in the UK.

EUROPEAN PROJECT

When the idea of European unity was born, a key reason was the understandable wish to avoid the horrors of yet another world war.

It seems that there are two broad opinions about the peace-based argument for European unity. Those against it can point to the special, and no longer current, factors which lay behind both World Wars as summarised in the chapter dealing with and responding to Remainers claims. Those in favour can say that such factors are mere hair-splitting and certainly did not occur to Churchill when he had a favourable opinion about post-war European unity no doubt based on vast experience of human folly and his maxim "Meeting jaw to jaw is better than war!"

The EU has definitely undertaken more than enough meetings to satisfy anyone wishing for "jaw to jaw" yet internal conflict continues relentlessly. Some say that the obsession with keeping the troubled euro is actually risking the peace due to its bad and unnecessary economic results such as high unemployment in the southern countries of the EU. Only time will tell whether the continuation of the EU will keep the peace or whether a Brexit-induced collapse of the EU would be followed by war.

The six original members of the European Economic Community (EEC) came together under the 1957 Treaty of Rome: France, West Germany, Italy, Luxembourg, Belgium and The Netherlands. The sheer divisiveness of the European Question had long since come to the fore by 1961 when an application was made by the UK to join the EEC. It failed due to the veto exercised in 1963 by the French President Charles de Gaulle amid fears that English would become the language of Europe and that the UK was not ready to become a member.

And so it all began, with cheers in the Commons from some and cries of "Shame!" from others: a foretaste of future conflict. The PM, Harold Macmillan, was acutely aware of the UK's privileged voice in Washington and he wished to ensure continued UK global influence despite the loss of Empire, i.e. by being heard in the US on European matters and in Paris and Bonn on US matters. He felt that the UK could play an effective role in the EEC. National confidence was then still suffering from the blow to UK prestige caused by the outcome of the 1956 Suez Crisis. De Gaulle vetoed another application in 1967 but had resigned by 1969. It is clear that governments of the 1960s saw very strong political advantage in UK membership.

Ted Heath, PM for the new Conservative Government, came on stage next with a strong desire to join the EEC but no wish to have a referendum. By 1973, he had negotiated entry to what was usually referred to as the Common Market. Harold Wilson, PM for the new Labour Government, went on to hold a membership Referendum in 1975. There was already strong UK opposition to the EEC within the first two years of joining! When asked "Do you think the UK should stay inside the European Community (Common Market)?" some 67% said "Yes". Since the Common Market had been sold to the people as a beneficial trading bloc, many were later unhappy when they finally realised that the true purpose of the 1957 Treaty was full political union. In those days, most of the Labour MPs were Eurosceptic.

In 1981, a splinter group was dissatisfied with the leftward direction of the Labour Party. They formed the pro-EEC Social Democratic Party led by the Gang of Four: Williams, Rodgers, Owen and Jenkins. In his left wing manifesto for the 1983 General Election, Labour leader Michael Foot promised a withdrawal from the EEC, but resigned after a landslide defeat. By 1984, Conservative PM Margaret Thatcher had achieved the famous rebate by threatening to withhold UK contributions to Brussels. In 1990, when she opposed extra power for the EEC including the common currency and made her "No! No! No!" speech to the Commons, many pro-EEC Tories were outraged. Indeed, her increasingly anti-European stance was key to her downfall and the accession of John Major that year.

The UK duly joined the Exchange Rate Mechanism (ERM) which was a sort of diluted common currency. On Black Wednesday in September 1992, there was panic in the London currency market and the Government failed in its efforts to support the pound: £10 billion spent from the reserves and an interest rate increase to 15%. The UK was ejected from the ERM.

We never did join the Eurozone and its euro currency at a later date. However, the ejection and the decision to keep the pound is now regarded by most as a blessing and the floating pound has proved very good for trade and the economy. Certainly, international economist Joseph Stiglitz has pointed out that a big problem with the euro is that it has removed freedom of action from Eurozone countries in recession. They can no longer decide to devalue their currencies, reduce their interest rates or adjust public spending, thus losing their economic sovereignty to the Troika of the European Commission, The European Central Bank and the International Monetary Fund.

Although Major won the 1992 election, by 1995 he was saying to his MPs "back me or sack me" over Europe. There was an ongoing rebellion by some Tory MPs over the increasing political union embodied in the controversial Maastricht Treaty which enabled the euro and brought in the new name of the European Union. It also gave Europeans the right to live, work and vote in any member state. He won that contest but lost the 1997 General Election to Labour under Tony Blair who went on to build more ties with Europe. When the existing national currencies of the Eurozone countries were discontinued in January 2002, the euro went into circulation. Ten more countries, Cyprus, Estonia, Hungary, Poland, the Czech Republic, Slovenia, Latvia, Lithuania, Malta and Slovakia, became members in May 2004, bringing the total number up to 25. It was a huge enlargement.

Even this short review, of the period following the 1957 Treaty of Rome, shows that the European Question has been toxic to UK Prime Ministers ever since. These are true lessons from history.

So far, we might say that the UK has long had a great sense of patriotism, national identity and pride. Since 1961, there has also been a very damaging conflict of opinion about the European Project within both main parties and their voters. Although Labour MPs have generally changed from Eurosceptic to Europhile since the Wilson Referendum of 1975, that comment applies much more to the Party than to the average Labour voter, as proved by the 2016 Vote.

In essence, a typical Eurosceptic could see no good reason to transfer a large part of British sovereignty to a much bigger and unaccountable entity on the other side of the Channel. But EU supporters claimed Britain was better off in the EU. Since over 70% of MPs were in this camp, Westminster has been accused of being "very much out of touch" with the people. On the other hand, MPs have long been suspected of being "very much in touch" with the career opportunities of the EU.

The opposing views and feelings inside the Conservative Party were major reasons why the PM bravely decided, or gambled, that the people should have their say in a referendum if the Party won the May 2015 General Election. Equally, there was a calculation that, apart from healing the Party, the offer of an In-Out Referendum could be a vote-winner. Hence, voters knew that they could vote on continued UK membership of the EU if the Tories were returned with an overall majority. In addition, it was made clear that the PM would negotiate reforms with the EU after the General Election and the detail of those reforms would be available to voters for the subsequent referendum.

In contrast to the predictions of the opinion polls, the Party was indeed returned with an overall majority, so enabling the Referendum. The Tory Manifesto offer of a referendum, only available in more limited form from Labour, may have been a key factor in the Conservative overall majority. That offer was clear whilst the Labour referendum offer referred only to future transfers of powers to the EU. The Labour leader, Ed Miliband, did not expect that in the event of a Labour victory in 2015, circumstances would ever cause his offer to be activated.

In the event, many felt that the PM's negotiated reforms were completely inadequate, so leaving the damaging division unhealed. Again, the pollsters predicting Vote Remain were confounded in the same way as for the 2015 General Election: they simply got it wrong. For example, Ladbrokes admitted that Remain was rated a 90% certainty as the polls closed. Vote Leave won the day with strong support crossing party lines. There is more detail on the history as it affected PM David Cameron in the chapter on the Day After.

CONCLUSION

Did the island history of Great Britain and her sense of national identity have a crucial impact in the minds of most voters? Or did Vote Leave mainly represent a slap in the face for a Westminster that was out-of-touch? Whilst it is most likely that Brexit resulted from a variety of causes, nobody could reasonably rule out the historical one.

With the force of history still in mind, now may be a good time to look at how the case was made for Vote Leave.

6   Vote Leave Case

"Smile at us, pay us, pass us; but do not quite forget;
For we are the people of England that never have spoken yet."

G. K. *Chesterton*

BACKGROUND OF UNCERTAINTY

This chapter, and the one about the Vote Remain Case, should be read in the light of a common feeling from all sides that there was a great lack of information, so making it difficult to reach an informed opinion. Time and again, although members of the public remarked that the Referendum was very important and that they wished to be told about the pros and cons of Leave and Remain, an absence of hard facts prevailed. Somewhat illogically, despite this lack, there was no shortage of strong opinions!

Whilst voters must make a considered judgement in a normal election, the Referendum was different due to various unknowns and the lack of manifestos. The usual guide of Left and Right did not apply because MPs of the two main parties were seriously split, as were the public. Officially, although both parties supported Vote Remain, a lot of traditional Tories and Labour supporters recommended Vote Leave. At times, both campaigns were caught "being economical with the truth," so generating low credibility. No-one really knew what the EU or the UK would do in the event of a Leave Vote.

We might call this the Uncertainty Issue which perhaps reached its most extreme form in the quote from Hilaire Belloc at the end of a bloodthirsty poem for children. Here is the last verse which followed the killing of Jim by a lion. A Cautionary Tale indeed.

> *"When Nurse informed his Parents, they*
> *Were more Concerned than I can say:—*
> *His Mother, as She dried her eyes,*
> *Said, "Well—it gives me no surprise,*
> *He would not do as he was told!"*
> *His Father, who was self-controlled,*
> *Bade all the children round attend*
> *To James' miserable end,*
> **And always keep a-hold of Nurse**
> **For fear of finding something worse."**

The last two lines are in bold because this was the allegory whereby the UK was advised to stay with Europe to avert disaster. In other words, Leavers felt that Remainers were trying to frighten voters by using the Uncertainty Issue to stoke Project Fear.

LEAVERS' GENERAL CLAIMS

Inevitably, there is some repetition here with the chapter on Perceived Need. However, for this one, the other side's responses are given below in italics in the same fashion as for the responses to Remainers' claims earlier. Since the claims and responses have been so hotly debated, it is likely that my understanding of the views taken will not always match the reader's recollection. If so, apologies in advance. Furthermore, the responses often fail to deal with the claims.

If Great Britain was not a member of the EU, why join today?

All voters should ask themselves this question because if the answer is "No," they should Vote Leave. The UK decision to join in

1973, as ratified in the 1975 Referendum, was based, for trading reasons, on being part of a Common Market which then had just six members. In 1975, those members were still the same as in 1957 many years earlier: France, West Germany, Italy, The Netherlands, Luxembourg and Belgium. However, in 2016, it is completely different because there are 28 members of a huge economic and political bloc with plans for further expansion and even more centralised sovereignty.

Key EU policies have failed: the euro as the Single Currency, the immigration problem both inside the EU and from outside the EU, and the over-regulation which stifles prosperity. Moreover, most of the members are subsidised by Germany and the UK. The worst example of dysfunction is Greece and its 50% youth unemployment not helped by EU enforced austerity. Its broken economy has been attributed by many to the failure of the "one size fits all euro."

Response: Whilst the EU is not perfect, it is best for the UK to work from within it to resolve its problems rather than quit. The overarching importance of the European vision of unity is much more important for Europe and the world than these problems. Freedom of movement and the euro must be kept because they are two of the EU's greatest achievements. It is far better to think of oneself as a European rather than a nationalist of one's country of birth.

Britain has no real influence in EU

All of the 72 measures, which the UK voted against in the Council of Ministers from 1996 to 2015, went on to become law. The Foreign Office said in March 2014: "By definition, if the UK is opposed on an issue that goes to a vote we are going to lose." It is incorrect to say that the UK's position at the top table should not be jeopardised because when it comes to a vote, the UK is permanently outvoted.

Response: The UK does have effective influence that would be lost in the event of Brexit. It is much better to work with our European partners to compromise and overcome all the issues than Vote Leave and take a "leap into the dark".

Although the EU is becoming ever more dysfunctional, it has no apparent interest in reform

There are serious problems which the EU shows no signs of wanting to solve thus risking the collapse of the whole European Project. For instance, if a country has to use the euro, it cannot adjust its exchange rate, so leading in some cases to very severe effects including high unemployment.

Another example is that many countries in Europe have a strong cultural identity of which they are proud. However, the EU seems unable to understand the deep anger created when people feel overwhelmed by the large-scale arrival of other cultures, whether from inside or outside the EU. The consequences of such poor policy can be drastic as when barbed wire fencing was erected by Hungary along its border.

Response: The euro and the free movement of people cannot be abandoned because they are the main achievements of the EU. Resources must be allocated to deal with any problems and this will work better in the future when the EU can raise its own taxes direct from its citizens. Free movement is essential to long term cohesion. It is right for example to expect Greece to abide by the "convergence criteria" under which the EU countries become economically closer. Austerity rules help this convergence process to the benefit of all.

Although most UK businesses do no foreign trade, they still have to comply with a mass of red tape from Brussels

Since many businesses are tired of being over-regulated without means of challenge, they see the Referendum as a chance to reform. The quote below is typical.

"At least with our own [government], I can chain myself to the railings at Downing Street," says Julie Price, an insurance broker. "With the EU, we've given up fighting."

Although less than 20% of UK businesses deal with foreign trade, they all have to comply with the over-regulation. It is unwanted interference from an unaccountable higher authority.

Response: There is a lot of merit in the so-called Red Tape because it protects working people by providing rights and satisfactory working conditions which they would not have otherwise. A consequence of Brexit would be the removal of this type of protection from the UK population.

The EU is unaccountable and run by bureaucrats who are anti-democratic and cannot be removed in any election

There are Presidents of the European Council, the European Commission, the European Parliament, the European Central Bank, the European Court of Auditors, the Court of Justice, and separately from these, there is a Presidency of the Council of the European Union. Apart from insiders, few understand it all except to say that there are appointments rather than elections. According to the film Brexit, The Movie, Brussels alone contains over 90 EU buildings. It is all an unaccountable and remote ivory tower.

MEPs are unable to initiate any legislation because that all comes from the Commission. Most in the UK do not even know the name of their MEP. It is impossible to hold anybody to account for bad government, e.g. the destruction of most of the UK fishing industry. Recent major failures in EU policy concern migration from outside Europe and the euro. In practice, there is no remedy for, or appeal by, member states except the drastic step of leaving the EU. The recent unsuccessful negotiation, with the EU by the PM, is a good example of the EU's arrogance and inflexibility. The UK will be much better off Voting Leave so that we can make all our own decisions and take back full control of our democracy.

Response: The EU is still a good way to bring nations together in a common goal of mutually beneficial improvements. Policies are widely discussed and agreed for the common good. MEPs can always have their say in the EU Parliament and much is safeguarded by the national veto system. The EU is the right sort of organisation to take forward the vision of more EU integration.

Vote Leave to take back control of the country including its borders

"I want my country back again" might be the case summary for the Leavers. Why give away your powers to an anti-democratic foreign entity? For hundreds of years, this country took all its own decisions, large and small. Whether it related to food regulations or a declaration of war, Britain was set up, as it should be, to carry out the wishes of her people.

A sovereign state can do anything it desires but a member of a wider super-state cannot: it is a tremendous loss of freedom. The UK is in a special position because it has a bigger history of beneficial laws and customs than other states. Thus it is jarring to think of relatively untrained foreign judges applying laws devised by unelected bureaucrats, and all a far cry from the relatively small customs' union which we joined in 1973.

But much worse is the EU requiring that there can be no limit on migration from the whole area of some 500 million EU citizens into the crowded UK with its existing overburdened infrastructure. It is a core EU objective which is soon to be enhanced in its effect by the entry of more countries including Turkey and its population of nearly 80 million. There has to be a limit and the only way of achieving that is by Voting Leave. Moreover, Brexit would mean a fair system of border control without discriminating against the rest of the world in favour of EU migrants; all would be subject to the same rules.

Response: Here are Little Englanders who think the country can survive on its own in the world without the benefit of the Single Market and its 500 million population. Let's not take a leap in the dark and instead, work with our European partners for the common good. The freedom of movement and euro are two of the great EU achievements and must be protected. They might have their downsides, but that is the price that has to be paid for the great European vision. Vote Leave would be followed by difficult trading conditions and other restrictions imposed by the EU which has to protect itself against other members wanting an In/Out Referendum. Exit terms for the UK would have to be harsh.

LEAVERS' SPECIFIC CLAIMS

Since the borders are completely open, it is not possible for the Government to plan the future provision of public services

Any country has to plan its public services with an eye to cost and the ability of the economy to generate enough taxation to pay for it all. There are both capital costs such as infrastructure, roads, buildings etc. and annual costs such as wages, heating, rents etc. Even in the unlikely event that all legal and illegal immigrants get jobs and pay taxes at the same rate as those emigrating, the increase in taxation cannot cope with the essential fresh capital costs like new schools and hospitals. Such extra costs are unaffordable at a time of record National Debt which will be difficult to service when, as they must, interest rates rise in the future.

Schemes like the new 646 bed £335 million Liverpool hospital, take years to plan and build. When no-one knows how fast the population will increase in future years, Government planning becomes impossible, so leading to Third World public services.

Response: All of the above is an exaggeration and there is no problem which cannot be solved by reversing austerity and providing adequate investment in public services. More to the point, immigrants are essential now to the public services because there are not enough non-immigrants willing and able to do this work.

Many migrants come from very poor countries and are happy to work for low wages, thus depressing the incomes of local people

The evidence is clear that both for unskilled and skilled work, wages have been depressed by the economic migrants. For instance, fruit picking, hotel work, plumbing and building have all seen lower wage levels become established at the expense of the existing workers.

Response: In line with the general theory of free trade benefits, this is good for the economy because costs are being driven down whilst the UK is helping poorer people from other countries. It is also essential for the UK to fill low-paid jobs with migrants because British people do not want to do such work.

The NHS is being overwhelmed by uncontrolled immigration

The NHS simply cannot support uncontrolled immigration due to the high cost of modern medicine and an ageing population. The evidence shows lengthening waiting lists for operations and poor performance in specialisms like cancer diagnosis and treatment. Perhaps most evident to the public, though not to most in Westminster, is the ever-increasing difficulty of getting a GP appointment. The English GP Patient Survey, quoted by the BMJ, showed that fewer patients in 2013/14 were able to book an appointment at their first attempt than in 2011/12. In addition, fewer found it easy to get through to someone at their surgery by phone and fewer had a good experience overall with the surgery. Without knowing the future number of patients, it is impossible to plan a reasonable service.

Response: the problem with the NHS is purely the ill-conceived austerity policy and to blame immigrants is racist. The Government should invest more in the nation's healthcare.

EU incompetence facilitates economic migrations from Africa and the Middle East

UKIP published a controversial poster headed Breaking Point. It shows Syrian refugees along the Slovenian border. The EU is said to have "failed us all," and "we must break free of the EU and take back control of our borders." Farage claims it is the truth that should be conveyed to voters. According to him, there has been no effective EU policy to stop or even slow down migration. The huge inflows are not made up of refugees or genuine asylum seekers but of economic migrants who are far too numerous to be absorbed by the EU.

The mixture of the German Chancellor making the big mistake of welcoming them and other countries like Hungary, trying to keep them out with new barbed wire fences, has just not worked. Many have reached the UK illegally mainly from France, and immediately disappeared into the black economy. Such big flows of humanity can easily hide terrorists who would do us harm. Whatever the BBC and the liberal intelligentsia might say, the British people understand that this sort of immigration is bad for the country. Brexit is the only way to regain control.

Author's note: This poster may be the most controversial part of the whole campaign and was opposed by the official Vote Leave group. Was it persuasive or counter-productive?

Response: Here we have more racism from the Brexiteers and probably it is the worst example of all. These people in the photograph are desperate and need our help. They want to come here and work for a living to help both themselves and the UK. It is heartless and unnecessary to discriminate against them in a bigoted way. Multiculturalism has been and will continue to be a great benefit for the UK.

Education is known to be failing because many schools' results are very poor. Why? – The huge influx of different nationalities speaking different languages

There is no good reason why the UK should suffer the big disadvantage of having to admit all and sundry. In a globalised world, it is essential to maintain our competitiveness starting with effective education.

In a Daily Echo article (12 January 2014) covering the hard-pressed St. Mark's School, Southampton, the paper describes a positive story of coping, involving a good Ofsted report in 2012 despite having pupils speaking 47 languages. It is good that both teachers and pupils have embraced multi-culturalism. The Head explains that they have children arriving from all over the world who are coming and going all the time. It is thus not simply to do with the EU, although 20% are from Poland. Whilst the school has evidently coped well with its difficult situation, as result of immigration, it is at the bottom of the Southampton league table and only half the pupils reach national targets for the three Rs. Is this fair on the ordinary British pupils?

Response: There should be no limit on immigration which is a great benefit to the country. Industry especially is keen to have low and semi-skilled labour having a good work ethic. Cultural diversity should be celebrated as a way of changing the UK for the better. We now live in a globalised world that is not interested in petty nationalism but moving forwards to an era of more tolerance and greater peace. Population movements like this are good for the UK and the world.

Millions are very unhappy at the restriction in choice of schools

In the past, parents have been able to rely on their children going to schools of their choice because the number of schools was adequate for the population.

Now, the uncontrolled explosion in the population has meant schools are hard-pressed and often unable to meet demand. There have been parent demonstrations with multi-coloured home-made placards reading "I don't want to travel for three hours a day" and "we want local schools." It is highly frustrating to be told that the good school up the road is fully subscribed so that your child must go to a poorer one several miles away.

Response: This is a false argument because the real reason for the lack of school places is the austerity policy and the failure of the Government to plan its investment in education properly. However, strenuous efforts are being made to supply more schooling and overcome the issue.

Housing is coming under unsustainable pressure from immigrants

There is already a huge UK housing shortage which means that it is impossible properly to absorb net immigration of around 300,000 p.a. together with the unknown extra number of illegals. Existing free movement rules of the EU permit any of the EU citizens to move to and reside in the UK. There are many cases of local people being unable to secure public housing because of homeless immigrants having priority. Excessive immigration has simply removed a key public service from the population. Also, much housing squalor exists as described in this extract from the Sunday Express of 4 October 2015:

"Squalid evil slums: What immigration is doing to Britain
Forty Romanian men women and children are crammed into a damp three-bedroom house, sleeping on mattresses in every room including the toilet. The

husbands are forced into slave labour on building sites and farms while their families struggle to survive on crisps and cereals from a makeshift larder in the attic."

Brexit would allow only those passing an Australian-style points system to enter the country. The borders really do have to be controlled to let in only the people who will benefit the country.

Response: This is racism and bigotry. Actually, the big influx from the EU has been beneficial because it fills the jobs that are needed to be done and which British people do not want to do. Where would the NHS and tourism industry be without all its foreign staff?

EU legislation is extreme and unnecessary causing all member states to suffer a loss of competitiveness

Perhaps because the EU is above all an administrative bureaucracy, it has created an incredible number of rules and regulations. Some of these (Directives) have to be enacted to a set deadline by member states in order to achieve a certain result. The means of achieving the result is left to members. Others (Regulations) are self-executing and thus require no enabling legislation by member states.

Many examples of over-regulation have a common thread of being time-consuming and in restraint of trade. For example, fruit must conform to a fixed specification before it can be sold thus creating extra work for the industry whilst requiring a lot of perfectly good fruit to be scrapped. Here is just one example relating to the definition of slight russetting:

"slight russetting such as

> *Brown patches that may go beyond the stem or pistil cavities and may be slightly rough and/or*
> *Thin net-like russetting not exceeding 1/2 of the total fruit surface and not contrasting strongly with the general colouring of the fruit and/or*
> *Dense russetting not exceeding 1/3 of the total fruit surface while*

Thin net-like russetting and dense russetting taken together may not exceed a maximum of 1 / 2 of the total surface of the fruit."

The purpose of this extract about russetting is to give an idea of the burden of the minutiae. It is from page 4 of the document headed:

COMMISSION IMPLEMENTING REGULATION (EU) No 543/2011 of 7 June 2011 laying down detailed rules for the application of Council Regulation (EC) No 1234/2007 in respect of the fruit and vegetables and processed fruit and vegetables sectors. CONSOLIDATED TEXT: Annex I; Part 1 of Part B MARKETING STANDARD FOR APPLES.

It is this sort of unnecessary and anti-competitive interference which has held down the nations of the EU over the years and partly explains their poor growth compared to the rest of the world.

Response: It is actually valuable to have a good framework of regulations in order to maintain and where need be, raise standards to the benefit of all.

The EU is so corrupt that its auditors have not been able to sign off the accounts for some 20 years

A Full Fact analysis of historical European Court of Auditors Statements of Assurance on EU budget is illuminating. It contains auditors' opinions on the reliability of EU accounts and legality/regularity of payments. From 1994 to 2006, the accounts were "not entirely" fair and accurate. From 2007 to 2014, they were described as "clean". For the entire period investigated, from 1994 to 2014, payments were not free from material error.

It is scandalous that these accounts are never correct such that taxpayers' money is simply disappearing.

Response: Since 2007, the accounts have been found to be accurate and reliable although there have been some errors in how money has been paid out. The Brexit claim is greatly exaggerated.

The EU costs UK taxpayers £350 million per week

The Brexit Battle Bus toured the country claiming in large letters that the £350 million weekly contribution sent by the UK to the EU could be used in the NHS. To do so would enable, for example, a new hospital to be built every week. Although you can argue about exact figures, the fact remains that the EU is very costly to the UK.

Author's note: I think this may be the second most controversial claim, after the Breaking Point poster, in the whole campaign. Farage distanced himself from it after the Vote, describing it as a mistake by the official Vote Leave group.

Response: The picture shows a plain lie on the Brexit bus. Of the £350 million in 2015, a rebate is applied at £100 million so that the true figure is £250 million actually paid. Of the £250 million, £90 million was spent in UK by EU allocation and just £160 million used as the UK contribution to the EU. The notice on the Vote Leave bus is extremely misleading and should never have been allowed. In a televised debate, one Remainer shouted across to the panel of Leavers: "Take that lie off your bus!!"

DID THE STRENGTH OF ARGUMENTS WIN THE DAY?

Some say that democracy is about the competing claims of the two sides with the outcome dependent upon the slightly mystic average will of the voters. On this basis, if the majority lean to one side, that must be the better bet for the country because the pros and cons have been properly weighed.

Perhaps unfortunately, it does not seem to be that simple. There is such a thing as populism which can work for anyone who is skilled at self-promotion. A good example is the mass support for Hitler from people who were to a large extent unaware of what he wanted to do.

The question becomes: "Did Brexit follow the arguments or the side with better campaigning ability?" It is explored in the next chapter.

7   Campaign

"The hardest thing about any political campaign is how to win without proving that you are unworthy of winning."

Adlai Stevenson

INTRODUCTION

How important are tactics in securing the desired result? Would there have been a very different outcome had the Remain Side shown more acumen? To help consider, rather than give clear answers to such questions, this chapter reviews the struggle from the viewpoint of both Leave and Remain.

Before doing this however, it is worth taking a moment to consider the great amount of hurly-burly during the whole campaign. Although it could not have assisted the cool consideration by voters of all the contentions, it hopefully gave no unfair advantage to either side.

Voters were bombarded through the media in two main ways: firstly, with claims from one side, and secondly, as a two-sided debate. Claims from one side were steady and persuasive whilst the debates became emotional. Although these debates should have given real balance and clarity, that did not apply very often because of the sheer noise.

Responses frequently did not answer the actual claims, so leaving the voter no wiser about the validity of the claims. This has already been evident in the chapters giving the responses to the arguments. It is the politician's method of not answering the question but going on to make a statement of his or her own. Moreover, the Uncertainty Issue was one reason for the "Yes it is; no it isn't" style of unhelpful discussion.

LEAVE SIDE

Although I have referred to Vote Leave generally in this book as the movement to leave the EU, in this chapter, the expression means the officially recognised body known as "Vote Leave."

From the start, there was rivalry and discord when Vote Leave, backed by Tory Eurosceptics, fought with Leave.EU backed by UKIP for the right to be the official Leave campaign. Whilst the former became officially recognised and the latter played a big part anyway, it was a rather fragmented opposition to the EU. Yet despite such division within the ranks and the thinly-veiled dislike between UKIP and Vote Leave, the Leavers won the day. Indeed, the disadvantage of division should not be overplayed because Vote Leave did go along with the Farage position on some key aspects, e.g. the idea of an Australian-style points system to control immigration and the warning about millions of Turks arriving in the UK. For his part Farage constantly said he wanted to work with Vote Leave.

By any standards, the Leavers were indeed the underdogs throughout. It is a word rumoured to derive from the days of sawing logs by hand when two men vertically operated a long two-handled saw, one at each end. The timber being placed over a sawpit, the man in the pit was the underdog and suffering from clouds of sawdust; the man at the high level, guiding the accuracy of the cut, was "top dog".

Leavers had arrayed against them the full force of politicians, big industry, banks etc. But unlike the underdog sawyers of old, Vote Leave may have wanted it this way as a strategy, appealing as it does to British sympathies for the less fortunate. Their campaign was operated by the highly experienced Matthew Elliott and Dominic Cummings, who brought to bear personal knowledge from two successful battles – to stop the UK joining the Eurozone in 2003 and to fight the Liberal Democrat plan for the Alternative Vote, defeated in a 2011 referendum.

One poster stated:

"We can make our own laws.
Our laws should be made by people we can elect and kick out – that's more democratic."

A key part of the strategy was to focus on democracy and sovereignty and to keep repeating Take Back Control, words which always seemed to be related to uncontrolled immigration. It worked because, against the expectations of many on both sides, this became a very popular catch phrase which sank into the public consciousness. However, it did not just happen. The reason for it was the discovery by Vote Leave that "forgotten England" was the key battleground. Extensive polling had established that huge numbers of Labour voters felt threatened by uncontrolled immigration, resented the EU and considered themselves abandoned. Distant from London, they had seen little prosperity. In a way, the message was: Vote Leave and be part of the people's campaign against the elite.

However, promotion of the sovereignty and democracy argument was not all plain sailing. Neither Vote Leave nor Farage's Leave.EU had access to party lists of voters. They also were not able to arrange as many events as the Remain Side. On the other hand, the Remainers appeared to be talking down to people and to be relatively smug. It may be that this impression, of the Remain Side being top dog, suited the Leavers' preferred underdog image very well because it meant that voters felt pressured to Vote Remain by the rich and powerful. If so, such a pressure was never likely to be well-received.

A second part of the strategy was the fear-based issue of Turkey and its population of nearly 80 million joining the EU and then having full freedom of movement to the UK. It was a single issue which concentrated the voters' thoughts on a number of worries at the same time: economic migrants, refugees, asylum seekers, hidden terrorists, EU free movement policy, trust in the EU to be competent and trust in the Remainers being truthful about the accession of Turkey being delayed until AD 3000. Thus, although Leavers were saying Remainers were using Project Fear, they were doing the same thing.

A third useful tactic was the infamous claim that £350 million per week of UK taxpayers' money was being lost to the EU, money which would allow a new District General Hospital to be built at the rate of one a week. Why not leave the EU and redirect the cash to the NHS? The real point here may be that despite virtually no-one in the end believed the claim to be accurate, voters thought that even £200 million per week was still an awful lot of money to send to the EU.

Apart from the use of strategy, Vote Leave produced solid tactics on the ground. In the earlier approach stage, thousands of volunteers were pounding the pavements and holding local meetings. UKIP were doing the same, the persuasive though divisive Farage keeping a high media profile. For that matter, so did Vote Leave and its hardest and most charismatic hitter, Boris Johnson. Somehow, the antagonism between Elliott/Cummings and Farage did not seem to matter, perhaps implying that most felt their campaigns were overlapping but complementary. It was not a case of too many cooks spoiling the broth.

The last stage was the four weeks known as purdah before the Vote on 23 June 2016 when the Remainers were forbidden from using the Government machine to advance their cause. Once purdah had begun on 27 May, Vote Leave finally made their policy statements knowing that the Government would not be able to attack them. They also concentrated on doorstep canvassing to ensure a good turnout. There was even a computer application which allowed volunteers to share canvassing returns on mobile phones.

Turning to the website, Vote Leave's reasons must have resonated with numerous voters: taking back control of everything including immigration, matters now decided by the European Court and the spending of taxpayers' money. The latter could in future be based on UK priorities not those of the EU.

The anomaly for Remainers may be that the fragmented Leave Side, with its low level of support from the big guns, seemed to understand the main body of voters so well that the Leave turnout was maximised to good effect. But that advantage was not realised by the relatively out-of-touch Remain Side until after the campaign. Was that effect crucial to the outcome? I doubt that we shall ever know.

REMAIN SIDE

Although there was never much evidence of undue confidence in the outcome from Vote Leave, the same cannot be said for the Remainers. They liked the Cameron Deal arising from his renegotiation, his recommendation of it and the intervention of President Obama, i.e. a winning combination, or so they thought. Yet perhaps this confidence increased the underdog advantage of Vote Leave.

During the campaign, the Leave Side had successfully labelled the Remain Side as operating Project Fear, a term which rang true to many and stuck in the public mind. It certainly accorded with Chancellor Osborne's doom-laden predictions for Brexit. After his bluff was called by the voters choosing to Leave, they were proved right by the absence of the threatened emergency budget. Already, it appears that the Vote Remain campaign, known as Project Fear, was becoming a liability, perhaps because its forecasts of economic disaster were never credible.

Project Fear was also irritating too many voters and Remainers. One pro-EU minister was angry with Osborne, especially as he was not permitted to put his case as a Europhile. There was no positive case put for the EU at all in his judgement. It left Remain with a miserable package which had failed to be sufficiently frightening. Boris

Johnson made the telling point that the Remain Side was very negative because there was nothing positive for them to say.

The Scottish Referendum vote had been won by the Government adopting this tactic of disaster for the UK arising from its breakup. A similar win was the 2015 General Election and the claim that financially, Labour was totally irresponsible. So far, so credible. It seemed the right way forward for the Referendum. In the event however, the EU Referendum turned out to be an entirely different matter. Had the Remainers been more in tune with the country, they would have understood that difference and run a better campaign. When Cameron said that Brexit would put a bomb under the British economy, voters were probably not convinced. Even if they were, the Vote appears to show that the control and immigration issues were more important. A columnist in the Daily Mail actually said he would eat grass if necessary in order to regain our sovereignty.

Complacency must have been a factor as most of the opinion polls backed a Remain victory right up to the last minute. The In Campaign Ltd., Stronger in Europe, was expecting a ten point lead on the day of the Vote. Polls were successful insofar as most believed them, even leading to Leavers saying they had voted Leave but did not expect to win. How many optimistic Remainers and pessimistic Leavers did not bother to vote?

David Cameron was partly responsible for the failure of the Remain Side with his over-confident and mistaken assessment of the electorate which <u>was</u> worried about Europe, did <u>not</u> accept Project Fear claims and felt its genuine concerns had been <u>ignored</u> by Westminster for a very long time. A common opinion was that the rich elite, who were mostly Remainers, did not have to worry about the problems of employment, housing, schools and the NHS. Labour and Corbyn, a historically Eurosceptic leader, did not reach out effectively with its half-hearted campaign; had it done so, would that have made a difference to the average Labour voter? Possibly.

Some Remain publicity backfired as soon as it was known. For example, coverage was given to a statement by the Centre for Economics and Business Research saying that over three million UK jobs are linked to our trade with the EU. The response was that over five million EU jobs were linked to trade with the UK, meaning that the EU needed the UK more than the other way around. The message received by the average voter was probably that there was no real risk to UK jobs from Brexit.

The Cameron Deal failed to convince because it was easy to criticise: insufficient reform had been requested from the EU by the PM, and there was no real restriction on free movement. The emergency brake on welfare was also successfully dismissed by Vote Leave as miniscule. Meanwhile, since Corbyn wanted unrestricted immigration in stark contrast to a huge number of Labour voters, there was no clear message from that source on this major issue.

There was one relatively minor event which showed some lack of campaign skills by the Remain Side. A boat was sent up the Thames to the Houses of Parliament by the fishing industry in order to call attention to its large-scale destruction by the EU. The sad fate of the industry was a solid and clear-cut example of the detrimental effects that can result from the work of the Commissioners. When a rival boat of Remainers including celebrities shouted abuse, it enabled Farage to remark that it was absolutely disgusting of the rich to sneer at and attack the poor in this way.

The pamphlet, sent by the Government to all the households in the country at a cost of £9 million, was neutralised by Vote Leave stressing how wrong and unfair it was to use the Government machine for one-sided propaganda. It could even have been counter-productive for the Remain Side due to the traditional British sense of fair play.

So far, none of the above sounds like a winning strategy.

Turning to the Stronger In Europe publicity machine, the first video on the website gave the six main reasons to Remain. All but one made an economic case and the exception referred to the European Arrest Warrant. No mention was made of the problems of immigration or democracy.

Despite the huge Remain coalition of most decision makers and opinion formers, there were damaging tensions. Lord Rose, former Chief Executive of Marks and Spencer, was appointed Chairman, said that Brexit would cause wages to rise and then disappeared from view. The Corbyn side were suspicious of Labour figures working within the Remain Side campaign because they had previously supported rival candidates for the Labour leadership. The SNP were fairly low profile thus raising the charge that they failed to achieve a good turnout. It was not a cohesive affair by any means. Was the disunity of the Remain Side fatal to its ambitions?

CONCLUSION

An impartial consideration, of the effectiveness of the two campaigns, leads to the conclusion that Vote Leave achieved the better performance. Although both sides were disunited, perhaps the Remain Side's disunity was more obvious because of its relatively large array of powerful supporters whilst the Leavers seemed to complement one another. The big unanswered question must be: "Did the success of Vote Leave hinge on its better understanding of the average voter and thus its better campaign approach?"

However this may be, the Vote itself can be used to gain some fascinating insights into the thinking of voters, as shown in the next chapter.

8   Vote

"This right to vote is the basic right without which all others are meaningless. It gives people, people as individuals, control over their own destinies"

Lyndon B. Johnson

INTRODUCTION

Unlike a General Election, this was a single issue about whether or not to stay in the EU. Although there were arguments on both sides and estimates of dire future consequences, there were no party manifestos. The success of the Vote Leave campaign was considerable bearing in mind that both main political parties were advising Remain and that special pro-Remain factors applied to London, Northern Ireland and Scotland.

In the same way as for a General Election, the BBC reported through the night as results came through to the studio. At 4.41 am, David Dimbleby announced it was clear that the Leave Side had won.

SUMMARY OF VOTE

AREA	VOTES Million	TURNOUT	REMAIN	LEAVE
UK	33.55	72.2%	48.1%	51.9%
ENGLAND	28.45	73%	46.6%	53.4%
SCOTLAND	2.68	67.2%	62%	38%
WALES	1.63	71.6%	47.5%	52.5%
NORTHERN IRELAND	0.79	62.7%	55.8	44.2
LONDON	3.77	69.6%	59.9%	40.1%
SOUTH WEST & GIBRALTAR	3.17	76.7%	47.4%	52.6%
SOUTH EAST	4.96	76.6%	48.2%	51.8%
NORTH WEST	3.67	70%	46.3%	53.7%
NORTH EAST	1.34	69.3%	42%	58%
EASTERN	3.33	75.7%	43.5%	56.5%
WEST MIDLANDS	2.96	72%	40.7%	59.3%
EAST MIDLANDS	2.5	74.1%	41.2%	58.8%
YORKSHIRE & THE HUMBER	2.74	70.7%	42.3%	57.7%

TOP TEN LEAVERS

AREA	LEAVE	FOREIGN BORN	FIVE GCSEs (A-C GRADE)	AVERAGE HOUSE PRICE
BOSTON	76%	15%	62%	£135K
SOUTH HOLLAND	74%	14%	71%	£154K
CASTLE POINT	73%	3%	71%	£238K
THURROCK	72%	13%	62%	£210K
GREAT YARMOUTH	72%	6%	58%	£145K
FENLAND	71%	6%	69%	£147K
MANSFIELD	71%	10%	65%	£115K
BOLSOVER	71%	4%	68%	£103K
EAST LINDSEY	71%	4%	64%	£145K
NE LINCOLNSHIRE	70%	4%	67%	£115K

None of these are remotely posh or expensive areas inhabited by the much-quoted Metropolitan Elite. But all the signs are that most voters could see no net advantage to staying in the EU.

TOP TEN REMAINERS

AREA	REMAIN	FOREIGN BORN	FIVE GCSEs (A-C GRADE)	AVERAGE HOUSE PRICE
GIBRALTAR	96%	-	-	-
LAMBETH	79%	33%	82%	£455K
HACKNEY	78%	38%	73%	£455K
HARINGEY	76%	40%	75%	£437K
CITY OF LONDON	75%	24%	N/A	£775K
ISLINGTON	75%	37%	82%	£580K
WANDSWORTH	75%	32%	83%	£545K
CAMDEN	75%	42%	81%	£675K
EDINBURGH	74%	16%	84%	£192K
E RENFREWSHIRE	74%	5%	85%	£199K

In sharp contrast with the top Leavers, this table is dominated by London and its pro-EU stance.

BREAKDOWNS AND SIGNIFICANCE

Countries, regions and top voting areas of UK

The total number of voters was 46.5 million of which 33.55 million cast their votes.

England had the highest turnout in the UK and the highest percentage Voting Leave. Although Scotland and Northern Ireland voted as expected to Remain, to the surprise of many, 17 out of 22 areas in Wales Voted Leave. It reflected the Welsh Labour strongholds voting for Brexit in contrast to the less numerous but more affluent voters in Cardiff, who wanted to Remain. Swansea Voted Leave. The benefit to Wales of EU money, £4 billion since 2,000, did not prevent the success of Vote Leave which was consistent with the election on 6 May 2016 of six UKIP members to the Welsh Assembly.

The only one of the English regions to Vote Remain was London by a big margin of 19.8%. Despite this balancing factor, the winning margin for Leave in England was still 6.8%, compared to 3.8% for the UK as a whole. It has been widely concluded that the final Vote resulted from a major disconnect between Westminster and the people, between the Government and the governed.

Scotland may be regarded as a special case with its recent overwhelming verdict against becoming independent and thereafter, somewhat inconsistently, returning the Scottish National Party with a massive majority. Every single Scottish area voted Remain. However, apart from Northern Ireland and Gibraltar, there were no other special cases thus leaving a stark comparison between London Remainers and most of the rest of the country.

The areas of top Leavers were generally in more remote parts of the UK where house prices were fairly low and there appeared to be relatively few foreign born. However, the Top Ten Leavers' table does not make clear the arrival of many foreign agricultural workers in Eastern England. In Boston for example, the top voting area for Leave, there has been a huge influx of foreign workers over the last ten years. According to the 2011 census, that amounts to a bigger percentage of

Eastern European migrants than anywhere else in the UK. In Wisbech, about a quarter of the population is from Eastern Europe causing people to be unsettled due to pressure on health, schools and the jobs, which are mainly in agriculture and food processing.

It is a question of the level and speed of immigration being too high for public services to be able to cope. In one BBC report, a traditional bakers' business (over three generations in the family) in Peterborough had closed down after 136 years in the same premises. A new Polish delicatessen is now trading two doors along the street from the empty bakers' shop. Unfair or otherwise, there is local resentment. The significance appears to be Westminster has ignored the problems leading to a demand for border control and a high Leave Vote. As reported by those travelling the country during the campaign, it can be better to listen to people rather than simply look at the opinion polls.

Housing is under pressure because landlords in areas of high demand will typically let their three-bedroomed semi-detached properties to ten immigrants, each paying £60 per week. Whilst unemployment is below the national average, the influx from the EU since 2004 has enabled the local economy to change. It has meant a lot more jobs in harvesting and food processing but a much lower hourly wage. Some businesses have benefitted and some have failed. Social changes include both pressure on maternity services and nightlife. In brief, one cannot look at the Top Ten Leavers' table and say the Leave Side won in an area of few foreign workers.

London was the only English region out of nine to Vote Remain. It has a high percentage of foreign born people as well as the oft-derided so-called Metropolitan Elite. Whilst educational attainment was somewhat higher than in the areas of top Leavers, house prices were enormously higher. But it is still too simplistic to say that in the UK, the rich and educated were Remainers and vice versa.

The 96% Remain vote in Gibraltar was due to its unique relationship with Spain and the risk of that country trying to reclaim it in the event of Brexit.

Age of voters

Apart from anecdotal evidence about the "young wishing to stay in EU", the Sun carried out a polling day survey of 12,369 voters. The age group preferences are as follows:

	Leave	Remain
18 – 24	27%	73%
25 – 34	38%	62%
35 – 44	48%	52%
45 – 54	56%	44%
55 – 64	57%	43%
65 +	60%	40%

It is clear that the younger the voter the more likely he or she was to Vote Remain. Anecdotally, this may have been even more significant with many saying "all my friends are voting Remain as well." Was it down to groupthink? One young person was asked by a reporter if he had any doubts and said "No," but then could not give any reason for his voting Remain. It has also been found that there was no total difference between male and female because each gender voted 52% / 48% Leave / Remain.

Voting by party supporters

	Leave	Remain
Conservatives	58%	42%
Labour	37%	63%
Liberal Democrats	30%	70%
UKIP	96%	4%
Greens	25%	75%
SNP	36%	64%

The only surprises here concern the two main parties. Although the Tories were known to be divided, there was an unexpectedly large majority for defying the PM's party line of Vote Remain. As for Labour, many thought that ex-Eurosceptic Jeremy Corbyn should have been more enthusiastic in trying to persuade the Labour voters to Vote Remain. Since this was the official party line, most MPs thought that the 63% Labour Remain Vote was far too low. Thus, whilst many Labour supporters complained that Corbyn should have got much more than 63% to Vote Remain, few Tory supporters complained that Cameron should have got much more than 42% to do the same.

When did voters decide?

	Leave	Remain
In the last month, I decided to vote	41%	43%
In the last week, I decided to vote	22%	25%
On polling day, I decided to vote	9%	10%

These poll figures are of great concern because they point to extreme indecision or confusion across the country. Had the mind-set of the polling day deciders been a little different, could there have been a victory for Remain?

Leave Factors

The Times reviewed the demographics of as many as possible of the 382 local authority areas in the Referendum to try and identify reasons for the Leave Vote. It appears to be representative in that 378 was the lowest number of authorities included in the four areas of analysis below:

Education

Areas were divided into those of high educational level and those of low level. The test for "high" was whether over a quarter of the electorate has good GCSEs at least five graded A to C.

	Leave	Remain
139 high level	46%	54%
240 low level	83%	17%

Manufacturing

	Leave	Remain
148 areas of low manufacturing	42%	58%
232 areas of high manufacturing	86%	14%

House prices

Areas were treated as having high prices if their average was above £282,000.

| 75 areas of high priced housing | 28% | 72% |
| 306 areas of low priced housing | 79% | 21% |

Pay

Areas were again divided into those where average annual earnings were below £23,000 (low paid) and those above this figure (high paid).

| 69 high paid areas | 35% | 65% |
| 309 low paid areas | 77% | 23% |

Interesting though these figures are, they should be treated with caution because it is far from clear whether they are statistically valid. Whether the educational finding is a result of the influence of the pro-EU BBC and educational establishment or other factors could no doubt be debated for a long time. Intriguingly, most of the Leaver areas, 240 out of 379 areas, had a low level of education whilst the top ten Leaver areas had a high level as shown in the table above. And is it really the case that low-paid people, living in industrial areas where housing is cheap were the backbone of Vote Leave?

CONCLUSIONS ABOUT VOTING

Were the Leave Side right to describe the Remain Side as operating a dishonest and gloomy Project Fear? Were the Remainers right to say that the country could not survive outside the EU with its

Single Market? Faced with such an emotional barrage of arguments, it is not surprising that many had difficulty in deciding how to vote.

On the frequent occasions during the TV debates when there was an absence of hard facts, voters could only rely on opinions. As tempers of both the panel and the audience rose ever higher, they had to assess who was right based on "Yes it is", "No it isn't". The EU was unwilling or unable to give any clear guidance on what would happen in the event of Brexit. Yet more uncertainty was created by regular reports that it was holding back unwelcome news until after the Referendum, e.g. fresh calls for more UK financial support and more details about the plan for an EU army.

The EU was painted as power-seeking, high-spending, addicted to regulations, corrupt and arrogant by the Leave Side. The world outside the EU was painted as harsh and difficult by the Remain Side. A neutral observer could be forgiven for seeing merit in both campaigns. Only the Leave Side was able to argue for taking back democratic control of the country and its levels of immigration. The Remain Side could only argue for more of the same EU. Voters' motivations may have largely reflected pre-existing opinions based on their knowledge of the impact of the EU and, for older voters, what preceded it.

Perhaps the main conclusion is that the clear vote to Leave on the biggest turnout since 1992 showed the extent of the disconnection between politicians and people. After all, the vote for Brexit was decisive although all main parties (except UKIP) backed Remain. Although the Remain Side had better funding and support from MPs, experts, banks and big business, the people were not convinced.

Whatever the exact mix of motivations might have been in the country, this was indeed a powerful form of democracy in action. People were determined to have their say.

And so we reach the aftermath. After all the excitement, razzmatazz and passion, how did everyone feel the next day? Was it elation or gloom? Was it statesmanlike understatement from Leavers and passive acceptance from Remainers? Did most Leavers proceed to celebrate in a state of euphoric expectation of an immediate exit of the

EU? As can be seen in the next chapter, it really was quite a mixture and the arguments continued relentlessly.

9   Day After Review

"There is nothing either good or bad, but thinking makes it so."

William Shakespeare (Hamlet)

INTRODUCTION

The City of London and the bookmakers had supplied incorrect predictions whilst the same could be said for most of those from the pollsters. Nearly all were expecting a win for Remain. Maybe the bookmakers were carried away by the confident rhetoric of the Remain Side or did they feel Brexit to be unthinkable? At all events, the outcome had the greater impact because Brexit was a big surprise to the country as a whole.

Early results hinted at a victory for Remain with Nigel Farage getting close to conceding defeat. Newspapers of 24 June were making the same assumption and saying how important it was for the PM to re-unite the country within the EU. But once the truth became known, the most dramatic consequences unfolded very swiftly on the Day After, starting with the resignation of the PM.

In stark contrast to these consequences, it was realised that there would be no change whatsoever in day to day arrangements with the EU. The UK would remain a member, the PM would still attend summits and there would be some two years to carry out the technical work of settling terms of withdrawal. Meanwhile, politics and trade would continue as normal. It was a late realisation of a time scale which should have been more evident during the campaign. One hopes there were few voters expecting Brexit to be implemented within days of such a vote.

By reviewing the extensive TV coverage on 24 June and the newspaper coverage on 25 June, this chapter concentrates on comments, plans and ideas as at 24 June. As elsewhere, the comments in italics are generally giving the sense of the remark rather than always being verbatim.

PRIME MINISTER'S STATEMENT

David Cameron describes the Referendum as a giant democratic exercise whereby the will of the people must now be respected and delivered. He points out that there is no doubt about the result. Britain has a strong economy and although there will be no initial changes in travel, movement of goods and services sold, decisions must now be faced. The PM is clear about his view that that Britain would be stronger, safer and better off within the EU, but the priority now is stability during the period before a new Prime Minister is installed by next October. It would then be for the new leader to trigger Article 50 of the Treaty of Lisbon 2007. He calls on Remainers to help make Brexit work and repeats that Britain can survive outside the EU. There is no repetition of his pre-Referendum comment about Brexit putting a bomb under the economy.

Beyond the high black security gates at the end of Downing Street, car horns hooted in celebration and an old man played Land of Hope and Glory on a hand-held organ.

NIGEL FARAGE'S DAY OF CULMINATION

For good or ill, depending on your viewpoint, Farage has been working relentlessly towards Brexit for 25 years despite only becoming

Chairman of UKIP in September 2006. After he was elected as an MEP in 1999, he became a thorn in the side of the EU Parliament and its pro-EU membership. His vow was to secure the exit of the UK and thereby be happily declared redundant from his job at Brussels.

UKIP had won the 2014 EU election securing 24 MEPs, an increase of 11, Labour achieved 20 (+7) and the Tories only 19 (-7). But there was much less success for UKIP at the 2015 General Election due to the British first past the post system. Thus, having obtained more than a third of the number of votes cast for the Conservatives, UKIP had one seat compared to 331 for the Conservatives: a rather frustrating outcome.

Around 10 pm on 23 June, Farage conceded that "it looks like Remain will edge it." He told the Daily Telegraph around 11.30 pm that the Government decision, to extend the registration deadline by two days to 9 June enfranchising another two million voters, could have helped Remain but that a victory for Remain at 52/48 "sounds about right. Who knows?" The extension had been justified by the inability of the computers to handle the many late applications to register by 7 June. However, it was controversial because of claimed bias, the late registrations being mainly by younger people supporting Remain. That said, reports from 10 June indicated just 437,000 extra registrations.

After the Sunderland result in favour of Leave and others showing a consistent pattern, Farage announced at 2.30 am "I now dare to dream that the dawn is coming up on an independent United Kingdom." A jubilant UKIP leader declared at 4 am, tears streaming down his face, "If the predictions are now right, this will be a victory for real people, a victory for ordinary people, a victory for decent people." It was understandably emotional, possibly enhanced by his winning bet on the outcome turning £1,000 into £3,500!

On 24 June, a senior Vote Leave source made clear that Farage would not be part of the cross-party committee negotiating Brexit despite the commonly held opinion that it would never have happened without him. Moreover, UKIP still has the largest British group of MEPs. No doubt his controversial Breaking Point poster, which was felt to have scared off moderate Leavers, had not helped relations. He was furious explaining that although he had wanted to, it was not possible to work with "these people" on a common agenda. Yet there was no denying Nigel Farage's personal triumph on 24 June, a day he celebrated with a breakfast of kippers and champagne! He proceeded to lead calls for the resignation of the PM.

POST VOTE TIMETABLE

23 June 2016

10 pm   Voting closes. Last on-the-day poll from YouGov had indicated 52/48 win for Remain and Ipsos Mori, carried out on 22 and 23 June, had said 54/46. But a secret poll for Leave.EU correctly predicted a win for Leave at 52/48. Although it covered 10,000 responses, it seemed to get generally ignored. Cameron was convinced of a win for Remain. Bookies agreed offering odds of 3/1 against Brexit. Official Vote Leavers cancelled their victory party.

12 pm   Newcastle-upon-Tyne returns 50.2% for Remain, lower than expected, so being the first hint of a Brexit victory.

24 June 2016

12.20 am Sunderland returns 61% for Leave, higher than expected. There was undisguised jubilation amongst Leavers. Later, Brexit votes were announced for Hartlepool, Basildon, Brentwood and Middlesbrough.

1 am   Swindon declares for Leave at 54.7% on a 76% turnout.

2 am   Jeremy Corbyn goes to bed to catch up on sleep.

2.15 am Arron Banks, founder of Leave.EU, claims victory. Later, Remain seemed to overtake Leave briefly with higher than expected figures from some areas e.g. Wandsworth at 75% for Remain. But Sheffield, which was expected to vote Remain, chose Leave at 51%.

4.15 am The West Oxfordshire win for Remain was at 53.6% but it was lower than anticipated and raised muted cheers only. Moreover, it was the area of the PM's constituency. Lancaster followed at 51% for Leave. By now, the outcome was pretty clear.

4.36 am ITV broadcast a win for Leave.

4.41 am BBC did the same.

4.45 am Boris Johnson phoned Michael Gove to arrange a press conference. The pound was down 8%.

6.03 am Leave achieved over 50% of the votes cast.

7.20 am The final result was announced in Manchester at 17,410,742 for Leave and 16,141,241 for Remain. It was 51.9% to 48.1%.

7.30 am Prime Minister Cameron phoned the Queen with his resignation.

8.20 am He made his statement to the Press outside 10 Downing Street.

As the result became clear, it was tears and huge disappointment amongst the Remainers in the Royal Festival Hall.

IMMEDIATE CONSEQUENCES OF VOTE

The Day After was extremely eventful making it difficult for everyone to keep up with the various momentous consequences of Brexit:

The emotional realisation that after 43 years, the UK would be leaving the EU
The hope that Brexit would prove beneficial.
Resignation of the PM.
Start of a Tory leadership contest to elect another PM.
Challenge to Corbyn's leadership of the Labour Party.
Stock market falls around the world including London.
Drop in value of £, against other currencies.
Political turmoil in the EU as leaders struggled to decide their reactions.

Apart from these definite results, a number of possibilities were the subject of endless speculation:

Another Scottish referendum for independence from UK?
Scotland joining the EU as a separate nation?
Border poll for a united Ireland?

New Tory programme in Parliament under new PM?
UK general election well before scheduled date of 7 May 2020?
Breakup of the EU as other nations became restive?
Fresh look by EU at policies including euro and immigration?

FOUR QUOTES FROM LOCAL PEOPLE

Having decided on Referendum Day to write this book, I made it my business to ask four local people here in the Bournemouth area for their one sentence comment on the Vote. Two were known Leavers and two known Remainers. These are their replies, verbatim, as received on 24 June:

Remainers:

"I hope those Voting Leave don't regret it."

"We are out, Cameron's out and I think it's chaos."

Leavers:

"We now have a fantastic, almost unbelievable, opportunity to steer our destiny and it may even drive Europe into a successful union without the undemocratic organisation that has developed over recent years."

"At last some common sense – now to make this country a benchmark for economic growth and social change. Look out world!"

IMPACT ON STERLING AND THE STOCK MARKET

Sterling reacted to Brexit with an early fall of some 11% to $1.32 to £ and 5.3% to €1.24. The fall was the greater because it reflected the fact that the markets had been expecting a vote to Remain.

The FTSE 100 Stock Market Index fell 4.75% to 6042 after an early drop of 8.5%. Banks and house builders were particularly affected with shares prices down at one stage by 35% and 40% respectively.

Again, perhaps in the light of the pollsters' and bookmakers' predictions of Vote Remain, the fall was all the greater. That said, other stock markets around the world had bigger falls. Meanwhile, the Brexiteers were unphased, pointing out the advantages of devaluation for UK exporters.

However, the FTSE 100 closed on 24 June 2016 at a reduction of 3.15% meaning that Britain's biggest companies had actually risen over the week of the Vote. Sterling ended the day down 7.9% against the dollar.

LOOKING BACK AT THE REFERENDUM

This section is a kind of post-Brexit post mortem. Many from both sides felt that there had been misrepresentation with voters being led astray. Leavers had always said that Remainers were operating Project Fear to frighten the voter. They now decided the Remainers were bad losers and re-christened them the Remoaners. There were calls for another referendum but these were angrily dismissed by the Leave Side asking the question: "What part of the word democracy do you not understand?!"

Although the margin for Brexit is just 4%, it is still decisive. More graphically, London and Edinburgh voted Remain but very few areas in between did the same. The country was divided, the generations were divided, and the rich and poor were divided.

A poll on Referendum Day by Lord Ashcroft reported on Leave voters' main concerns after they had voted. The first was loss of sovereignty and the second was immigration. Remain voters' main concerns were first the economy, jobs and prices, second access to the Single Market and third a feeling of isolation. Are these all fair comment or misconceptions? For instance, judging by the endless heavy criticism of all UK Government decisions, one might have supposed the EU could have done no worse! Or do we prefer to make our own mistakes thank you very much? As for the Single Market, there was a lot of confusion generally with many Remainers believing access would be simply lost, rather than would continue on possibly less favourable terms. Moreover, did the two sides ever really listen to each other?

There were recriminations. Some Remainers were angry that personal attacks were outlawed by No. 10. But the ban was no doubt perfectly proper on the grounds that such methods are no way for the country to take this immense decision. In one early TV debate, a Remain government minister had attacked Boris Johnson as being the life and soul of the party but not someone that you would want taking you home. The remark probably backfired and was not repeated. A Remain poster was designed, showing a mini-Johnson in the top jacket pocket of Farage; it was never used.

Some more general questions relate to the motivation of the Leavers and the democratic quality of the outcome. Were they unaffected by Project Fear because they felt they had so little to lose? Since their perceived problems of housing, jobs, schools and the NHS were not recognised by Remain, did the Leavers think that it could only get worse after a Remain victory? And was the result some sort of emotional mob rule which was not even democratic because the voters were grievously misled? But was it Leave or Remain which misled the most? Or alternatively, did the Leavers simply vote for future democracy without giving any thought to the EU as a force to prevent another European-wide war? If there had been any sign that the EU was prepared to become less arrogant and to reform, would they have voted in the same way? Difficult questions.

After the failure of the Government's alleged Project Fear and the Vote, there was a tide of publicity which became known as Project How Dare you? In keeping with the Remainers' theory that the voters had got it wrong, plans were laid for Project Damage Limitation. The Bank of England made a soothing statement about a new £250 billion facility for the banks, albeit Governor Mark Carney, a Remainer, was far too long-faced for the taste of the Leave Side. Leavers were naturally wanting a positive and confident attitude from the Bank, rather than the appearance and sombre tones of an undertaker. Certainly, his broadcasts came over as his solution to the unfortunate catastrophe of Brexit.

There were accusations of hypocrisy against the CBI which had been a strong Remainer predicting a cost to the economy of £100 billion and a million jobs. After the Vote, the CBI had a different story, one of confidence that companies would successfully adapt. There was a suspicion that if Remain had won, their supporters would have received favourable treatment in some way.

The greater short term uncertainty caused by Brexit was bound to have some adverse impact on an economy that was already slowing. The cost of living would have to rise due to the higher prices of imports and the country would appear less attractive and welcoming to immigrants in general. Nonetheless, the drop in the pound made UK exports more attractive to foreign buyers and the drop in interest rates meant reduced interest charges on the National Debt, both good signs for the UK. Stronger exports would feed through to more prosperity, jobs and spending power. Another benefit was the clear and immediate abandonment of Osborne's threatened austerity budget. Had that always been a false threat? Whatever the reasons, things stayed calm after the Vote and there was no real financial panic.

Naturally, there were winners and losers amongst the big companies. The former included exporters, food drink and tobacco sectors and miners of precious metals. The losers included banks, housebuilders and airlines. As usual, the market adjusted share prices immediately and companies must have already been re-planning their future.

One curiosity of the Referendum is that the main force, persuading both Labour and Conservative Parties to try and join the EEC in the 1960s, was never mentioned: the importance to the UK of having a powerful voice in Europe on behalf of, or in conjunction with the USA and in Washington, for Europe.

PRIME MINISTER AND HIS REFERENDUM DECISION

The result was a great shock to the PM who was convinced of a Remain Side win, a view partly based on private Downing Street polls. Perhaps it was the last great illusion after his failed placatory attempts to deal with the difficult European Question. In 2005, as part of his successful campaign for the Tory leadership, he had wished to appear both a moderniser and Eurosceptic. The latter was achieved by pledging to withdraw the Tories from the federalist European People's Party, a pledge only implemented after four years.

In September 2007, he had made a "cast iron" promise of a referendum on the proposed European Constitution as a further sop to the Tory Eurosceptic wing at Westminster. But that proposal was dropped after anti-constitution referendum results in France and Holland. As UKIP never tired of pointing out, whenever people in the EU had a chance to vote, they always voted against the EU. However, when the European Constitution was duly reborn virtually unchanged as the Lisbon Treaty, sceptics did not forgive the PM for claiming his promise no longer applied on the grounds that as it had become law in December 2009, the matter could not be re-opened. UKIP duly christened the PM as "Cast Iron Dave" whilst he called their members "loonies, fruitcakes and closet racists." The omens were not good.

The big internal Tory split on Europe grew in significance as the immigration and euro problems became ever greater. Meanwhile, the 2010 Conservative-led Coalition with the Liberal Democrats was a question of compromises, one of which was that there would be no referendum. In October 2011, 81 rebel Eurosceptic MPs pressed for a referendum anyway but were defeated in the Commons. Perhaps as a response to his critics, two months later the PM vetoed a rescue plan for the euro because it meant unacceptable loss of sovereignty. Although that move pleased Eurosceptics, the merit of the veto was much disputed. Even when making his Bloomberg speech in January 2013 pledging a referendum, Cameron tried to keep a foot in both camps by using the speech to argue for Remain.

Having, to his surprise, won the 2015 General Election with an overall majority, the referendum plan had to be progressed. Perhaps the promised referendum was key to that win. But when the negotiations were carried out with the EU, the latter had more pressing issues to confront, i.e. immigration, the economic crisis and terrorism. This probably prevented them giving the talks the attention which they deserved. Alternatively, their disinterest in engaging in the talks could have been due to Ivory Tower Syndrome. A very common opinion is that he had not asked for enough reform. At all events, his eventual renegotiation package was deemed to be insufficient by the voters.

And so the PM failed to get his way on the Referendum. One assessment is that he had always tried to manage the European situation rather than operate from conviction. Was he a soft Eurosceptic or an EU enthusiast? Nobody really knew. Had he failed because he made the misjudgement of trying to use management methods when the Referendum needed leadership? Was he simply a lucky politician whose luck ran out?

Harold Wilson had triumphed in the 1975 Referendum over the majority of his MPs who were Eurosceptic whilst Cameron failed despite having a big pro-EU majority on both sides of the Commons estimated at 490 of the 650 MPs, some of whom later said they would battle to scupper the vote by stopping the implementation of Brexit. However, the Wilson referendum was much simpler with just six nations in the EEC and no problems with terrorism, immigration or a common currency.

Mrs. Thatcher had no problem in supporting the Remain Side in 1975 before political union had become an issue. Unlike Cameron, Wilson had been correct in judging that he could appeal directly to the people of the UK to get what he wanted. But history could yet put David Cameron in the favourable light of having been the leader who enabled an essential national vote when it really mattered. It may have turned out as a lost gamble for him, but this time, it really was democracy and action, not just words.

When the PM, his wife Samantha standing to one side, gave his emotional resignation speech outside 10 Downing Street in the early morning of 24 June, there were tears both inside and outside the building; it was a very sad moment. Feelings in the country were more mixed. Whilst many were sympathetic, probably a similar number felt it was high time for him to go and for the vote to be implemented without delay. Some hopes!

LEAVE SIDE REVIEW

There were two different reactions amongst the leaders of Vote Leave: jubilation from Nigel Farage's UKIP and solemnity from the official Vote Leave members. Farage was delightedly claiming victory for his long anti-EU crusade in no uncertain terms. He was probably the most entitled person of all to make that claim after his relentless 25 year campaign. No-one had done more. Yet he was not popular with the official Vote Leave side who avoided any triumphalism or back-slapping at their press conference. Instead, Johnson, Gove and Stuart struck a fairly sombre note about moving forward towards Brexit in unity and in the interests of the whole nation. Some Leavers, including in particular Johnson, were upset at the resignation of the PM because they felt he was the best person to deliver Brexit. Farage strongly disagreed saying that Brexit needs a Brexit Government.

Celebrities, most of whom seemed to support Remain, used Twitter to publish their disappointment but got short shrift from Leavers. For example, when Gary Lineker said that he felt ashamed of his generation, one user wrote that it would be different if he lost his Match of the Day job. Presumably, that user had some involvement with migrants taking locals' jobs. When J K Rowling said she had never wanted magic more, the riposte was that sadly for her, she had got democracy instead.

A cartoon was published showing an aeroplane, marked European Union, steeply crashing to earth with its engines in flames. Several people have managed to escape from it and are floating down on parachutes decorated with the Union Jack. The pilot is shouting to them with the words "You guys are taking a huge risk." This picture demonstrates the feelings of many highly pleased Leavers. They did not buy the theory that Brexit means a huge risk; rather, they saw it as an escape from a doomed plane.

There now follow some quotes (mainly verbatim) from the winning side as a continuation of all the campaign remarks. It could be that they give a much clearer idea of the Leavers' attitudes of 24 June 2016 than can be gleaned from a descriptive narrative.

"The Chancellor's pre-vote claim, that there would have to be an emergency budget in the event of Brexit, has been shown to be a cynical ploy. The £35 billion mixture of tax increases and spending cuts will never happen and was never justified."

"The projected cut in pensions and an armed conflict in Europe were both scare stories from the Remainers and will not happen."

"So have you decided to listen now Mr. Juncker?"

"Leave had the mantra of Take Back Control but there was no straightforward message from Remain."

"Just because there could be economic problems with Brexit does not mean the economy would be any better under Remain."

"Cameron has been destroyed by Johnson and Farage."

"There's a proper people and proper economy going on in this country that David Cameron doesn't know about."

"Finally, the voice of those who have been ignored was heard."

"Europe lost Britain through its refusal to give Cameron a deal."

"This Vote is the biggest slap-down of the Establishment in history."

"There has been a reappearance of the patriotic element of Labour whilst the Blairites are on the run: very good too!"

"The main focus of the Referendum was immigration and the repeated failure of successive Governments to bring arrivals under control."

"This is Britain. We have been here for hundreds of years. We will sort it out like we always do."

"If we are buying 20% of EU produce, they won't turn round and say you can't have it. We will get it."

"Now it's Project Spite from EU cheerleaders."

"The Remain Side could provide no answer to the problem of immigration."

"The EU is now facing the worst crisis in its 59 year history."

"Our deepest tribal instincts have been roused by uncontrolled immigration and loss of sovereignty to unelected bureaucrats."

"The EU will now have to change its plan for a United States of Europe into a group of sovereign states."

"We have had enough of big government and big business telling us what to do."

"I voted to Remain because my mum told me to. I did it to keep her happy. It's not the best reason."

"The Single Market is a complete disaster for us. We have a huge deficit inside it."

"The vote could trigger a new spirit of entrepreneurism."

"Vote Leave were never anti-immigrant. They just wanted a colour and nationality-blind system which was planned so that we can organise schools, hospitals and housing to cater for a known level of immigration."

"We must remember something which is easy to forget. Brexit is the result of democracy and if we do not like the result, are we saying that we would prefer something else?"

"The PM should have come back from Brussels in February with a much better deal."

"The mother of parliaments will no longer be a shrivelled version of the democracies that she inspired."

"This is the third time that Germany has tried to rule Europe. Why should we be dictated to?"

"Except for London and Scotland, the conviction was that the political class has allowed unchecked immigration to change the very fabric and identity of Britain."

"Now we have a chance to make Britain, Britain again: a self-governing country with its own parliament."

"Labour and the Conservatives should now collapse and be replaced by parties which reflect the true divisions in the country."

"Cameron chose to have the Referendum and lost: that is why he is resigning."

"The regrets of the EU leaders about Brexit are hard to stomach. We wonder whether they also regret their stubborn refusal to compromise."

"The NHS must ensure that EU staff still feel welcome."

"There are more asylum seekers in Middlesbrough than anywhere else in the country. The Leave Vote of 65% reflected the fact that that there are so many non-English speaking children, the teachers' time is taken up trying to deal with them so that others fall behind."

"The UK vote is a calamity for Brussels."

"Brexit is a stinging message to the EU political elite."

"Brexit revealed austerity-weary frightened voters who want housing security and proper jobs."

"Boris has won it for Brexit."

"Listening to the other side, you would think that the Leave campaign was anti-foreigner or anti-immigrant."

"Today has been the best day of my life."

"It is about money. Immigration has caused the NHS and schools to be at breaking point. The UK pays into the EU and gets less out."

"I'm just glad we're out of it because this is our England. This is our England."

"We can't be bullied by Brussels."

"Bloody-minded insurgents are a vital part of our history. Now the 17 million Brexit supporters can join their ranks."

"Nothing will change in the short term."

"There is disillusionment with politics. Bring the Government to the centre of the country; all are getting sick of how things are."

"Like Marmite, you love him or hate him, but Nigel Farage gave us the chance to vote."

"The Brexit success has a thousand fathers written on its birth certificate including sneering Remain sophisticates, e.g. any narcissist with a man bag who characterised the British working class as wholly bigots, loudmouths, ugly chavs, racists and fools."

"It is a very good day for democracy and we now need to stand together."

"The EU has never been any good to us."

"Identity is a banner that people are prepared to risk economic destruction to protect."

"The EU was a great idea for trade but not politics."

"Unrestricted freedom of movement is psychologically unendurable for the economically insecure."

"I've got my country back. What I've got I want to keep."

"In two years' time, we will say Thank God for Brexit."

"Our island history now has a signpost taking us in a new direction."

"The British people have again shown an understanding of Nelson's remark: 'The boldest measures are the safest'."

Obvious signs of resentment outside the biggest cities had been ignored for years. For example, in 2013, people in Peterborough claimed that the agencies would only hire non-UK nationals in order to pay low money for long shifts. In Lincolnshire, new arrivals may have been optimistic, but locals were resentful. Jobs were precarious and homes hard to find.

The biggest issue, reflected more than any other at the polling stations, was probably immigration. Often consistent with this, massive majorities for Leave were delivered in traditional Labour areas, showing the remoteness of the leadership of the Party from its members. One UKIP activist in South Wales referred to the frustration of voters with politicians who did not limit newcomers when they themselves were struggling to find decent-paying jobs.

The performance of their stock markets in other countries gives an idea of how badly the Brexit Vote was received outside the UK. For instance, at one time in the morning of 24 June, the markets in Spain and Italy had dropped 10% compared to just 5% for London. This could be due to Brexit putting the UK in a relatively better place than other euro-damaged economies in the EU.

Brexit has a widely-held general explanation, one which is easily understood in terms of Victory for the Common Man. It runs something like this. Britain voted for hope not fear. In an act of daring, we ignored the "instructions of our betters" and the threats of Brexit causing another war in Europe, and stood up for our country. The majority personally knew of cases where an overstretched NHS had given poor treatment such as the pregnant woman who found her maternity unit full, became high risk due to two days' delay and then had a traumatic delivery. Or the nine year old boy in agony for 36 hours with appendicitis because there was not a single paediatric bed available in London over that period. Such examples are more plausibly explained by uncontrolled immigration than by a lack of investment in the NHS.

It was no good Remainers dismissing these examples as purely anecdotal because they struck a chord with the millions of mothers who were trying to get medical appointments and school places.

People refused to be falsely stigmatised as racist because they did not want their taxes sent abroad and did not want everyone in the EU to be able to migrate to our overcrowded country. In short, a very high proportion of voters did not take kindly to being reviled for their legitimate concerns and decided to Vote Leave.

Put another way, they were angry that for many years, the politicians had ignored a growing and stunningly obvious problem. When it could no longer be ignored, rather than take responsibility for their inaction, the politicians tried to insult their victims as bigots. There was no contrition; no-one admitted for example that you cannot have endless immigration without a proportionate increase in the size of the NHS.

There is another view or "take" on Brexit whereby it followed a peculiarly British and violence-free solution to the serious Governmental Problem of Lost Democracy. British voters had the necessary courage to go against the massed ranks of Prime Ministers, Presidents, politicians, economists, celebrities, the IMF, the CBI, bankers, bishops and the BBC. Being pro-EU is almost part of the CV one needs for top jobs whilst the idea of sovereignty is considered much less important than a seat at the top table. In the ordinary course of events, few can battle against such odds and such a high proportion of senior pro-EU decision-takers, even in the end, Margaret Thatcher.

But a referendum allows a battle because it is a single issue with each vote counting equally. It is beneficial high-powered democracy as witness the whole range of upheavals now happening due to Brexit. The masses actually realise that the EU means the loss of legal rights and the normal powers of self-government. By contrast, Prime Ministers have not properly stood up for Britain against the ever-encroaching powers of the EU.

Under this view, when Cameron reluctantly capitulated to democracy, people were at once determined to have their say at the ballot box. They chose freedom for the UK over the undesirable, progressive construction of an unelected super-state raising its own taxes directly, controlling the UK armed forces and becoming even more arrogant, detached and powerful. It was nothing less than the exercise of the deep cultural instinct of the people. Again, in the same way as for the Remain Side review, I would stress this is my sense of the argument only, not my opinion which remains undisclosed.

REMAIN SIDE REVIEW

The day after the Vote, there was wide coverage in the Press and on TV of a young woman covered in blood outside the Houses of Parliament. She was smiling and holding a home-made placard announcing: BREXIT: WHAT A BLOODY JOKE. An individual and personal expression of horror at the Brexit result. Although the blood streaming down over her head and T shirt was not real, it was certainly very realistic. Apart from conveying horror, the disturbing picture is also likely to be an extreme example of the anger shown by some Remainers.

Remainers were said to be literally "grieving" at the outcome. There was a clear impression that feelings in favour of Remain were so strong that many younger people were simply not prepared to accept the vote as a democratic outcome. The idea that the voters, not least the older ones, had got it wrong can be seen in some comments shown later.

Huge numbers gathered outside Boris Johnson's home in North London protesting against the Leave result. Although there were some cheers, it was mainly booing and swearing from those noisily unhappy about Brexit. Police ensured his safe passage through the crowds. Yet the Remainers may have drawn some comfort from his difficulties. These included a backlash when people realised that immigration was not going to be greatly reduced any time soon. Leavers would also become angry about the long delay before serving the Article 50 notice to leave the EU. The popular Boris was certainly not in for an easy ride.

Meanwhile, the Anyone But Boris (ABB) movement had many adherents in Parliament. Certainly, the PM in waiting appeared on TV as more thunderstruck than raring to go. Particular resentment may have resulted from him being probably the most charismatic politician involved in the whole debate, and one who may only have backed Leave to further his ambition to become PM.

After the predictions in favour of Remain, the disappointment felt by some was almost overwhelming. Anna Soubry, Business Minister, expressed her feelings of sadness on this "dreadful day which is the worst day of my life". In London, some 60,000 signed a petition calling on the mayor to declare the capital's independence and remain inside the EU. Although it was a tongue-in-cheek petition expected to secure just a few hundred votes, the large number of supporters is a measure of London discontent.

Since so many Labour voters backed Brexit and cuts in immigration, Jeremy Corbyn, who seemed to back unlimited immigration, was felt by most of his MPs to be out of touch and should therefore resign as leader of the party. For instance, Labour MP John Mann remarked that the Party had failed because it had not had the courage to face up to the immigration issue. Despite his campaign comment that he would give the EU only 7 out of 10, Corbyn disagreed, saying that he would not resign and claiming that the agenda now is to fight austerity. But party members still said that he should be called to account pointing out that the Labour leadership had given the impression of studied detachment during the campaign.

The so-called lacklustre approach was deemed so bad that reportedly, many Labour voters did not even know that Labour was pro-EU. Former leader Ed Miliband said as much on TV before the Vote. Nonetheless, it is a moot point in view of the blanket press coverage of the Referendum and the high turnout. It is very possible that they voted for Brexit in full knowledge of the official party policy but simply disagreed with it. MPs Hodge and Coffey duly prepared for a coup by submitting a motion of no confidence in Corbyn to the Parliamentary Labour Party (PLP).

More relevant could be the fact that most of the PLP did not support their leader anyway, seeing him as an electoral liability. He had become leader through the Electoral College system whereby most of the MPs had never voted for him. However, the PLP difficulty was that Corbyn's supporters claimed with good reason that any challenger would fail due to the leader's support from the votes of the left wing unions and party members in the country.

The Labour post mortem also conceded the Remain Side were far too negative with little said about the merits of the EU. Despite this assessment, the whole country would have to make the best of these new dangerous waters. The Labour Party said it should therefore be fully involved in the Brexit negotiations.

There was an immediate view after the Vote that Brexit is a monster having a whole batch of adverse consequences. Examples of it "touching and destroying" include the PM's resignation, the need for a new Tory leader, the challenge to Corbyn's leadership of Labour, the beginning of the end for the EU, the rise of extremism in Europe and the UK, the feelings of rejection suffered by EU immigrants, and the collapse of the pound and the stock market.

Some Remainers claimed that since the vote was achieved through misrepresentation by the Leave Side, there should be a fresh referendum possibly after further negotiations with the EU. The claim gained little traction however on the Day After. Another argument related Brexit to a huge loss of national stability by saying that questions had been raised about all of the five pillars of the UK: the political system, the legal system, the public finances, the openness for trade and the City of London.

Still others called for the majority of MPs on the Remain Side to use that majority to keep Britain in the Single Market whilst Leavers warned that such a move would spark a constitutional crisis. Another knee-jerk reaction was to point out that the large number of Remainer MPs could prevent the proposed Bill, to repeal membership of the EU, from ever becoming law.

The following quotes from 24 June 2016 provide a good idea of the Remainers' varying reactions to the Vote. There is a sense that unlike a General Election, many are just not happy to accept the outcome as a democratic result. Are the British becoming more intolerant generally?

"The message from Leavers, that immigration could be turned off like a tap, was a lie. The same applies to the projected saving of £350 million per week as stated on the Vote Leave bus."

"Although millions are joyous, there is now a new and uncertain future for a divided nation whose currency has just fallen off a cliff."

"The result has divided the country so that we have now become 'two nation Britain'."

"It is a slap in the face. Anyway, London is run by immigrants who do all the cleaning and manual labour."

"The truth is that the Conservatives' immigration policy is not credible and Labour have several immigration policies which were discussed at a seminar during the campaign. It was not ideal."

"The shock waves which have hit the City of London have yet to get through to the wider economy."

"Complacency in the City turned into shock."

"The Bank of England is concerned about the large uncertainty now prevailing and has allocated £250 billion in order to support the banks as necessary. However, the UK financial system is in good condition."

"I am ashamed of our country."

"The wrinkly bastards stitched us young 'uns up good and proper on Thursday."

"It was an unlikely alliance between Labour heartlands and shire counties."

Author's note: It may have been unlikely but the same occurred when the country felt threatened by World War I and there was no shortage of volunteers. Can that be compared?

"This will not be an amicable divorce."

"A 43 year bond has been broken."

"For me, as a lifelong English European, this is the biggest defeat of my political life."

"As an importer, I can say that Brexit is bad for business."

"Brexit means that our futures have been taken away."

"Young people have been betrayed by older people. I am literally shaking."

"Remainers did not supply enough facts about the economy and the security of the UK, so allowing these important matters to be trumped by fears over immigration."

"Small town Britain was not listened to and felt left behind."

"It was a lousy campaign by Jeremy Corbyn."

"I feel devastated and gutted."

"The Breaking Point poster was my breaking point."

"I feel like someone's kicked me in the stomach."

"It could result in violence."

"Brexit fills me with dread."

"The older voters have betrayed younger people and taken away their future."

In the same way that there was a view or "take" explaining the approach of the Leave Side, the Remainers had their own particular outlook, as expressed after the Vote. They appeared to stereotype Leavers as having one or more of a number of undesirable attitudes or elements: stupidity, bigotry, living in the past and a lack of care for younger people. Much of this is reflected in the comments above.

The Leave Side are also deemed wrong to think that the UK can survive outside the EU which will punish us for Brexit. We can now expect a loss of workers' rights, no access to the essential Single Market and no continuation of medical care arrangements for Britons abroad.

However, they were not able to contest that Brexit meant the return of sovereign power, nor could they complain about economic catastrophe because it had not occurred and did not even appear likely. Nobody was claiming any need for Osborne's threatened austerity budget.

Is it right to say that the Remainers were just bad losers? Probably not, because the view above is likely to be that of a vocal minority whilst most have accepted the democratic outcome.

WHAT NOW?

Having cast a decisive vote to the leave the EU, the people of the UK proceeded to imagine its future as an independent country without the benefits or disadvantages of membership. Again, all were not happy to accept and make the best of the democratic outcome.

10   Looking Ahead

"We are not permitted to choose the frame of our destiny,
but what we put into it is ours."

Dag Hammarskjöld

Having reviewed the outcome, the following comments show the start of the big post-Brexit debate and the first ideas that were canvassed as to the way forward.

There are plenty of things to ponder as at 24 June 2016, e. g. the undoing of the PM by his referendum gamble, the possible undoing of the Leader of the Opposition by his so-called half-hearted campaign and majority opposition to his leadership from his MPs, the need for an early indication of how Brexit will be managed, the risk of a breakup of the UK by the loss of Northern Ireland and/or Scotland, the final acceptance by all that Leavers cannot be stigmatised as racists or bigots, the need to address voters' legitimate concerns in the future and not least the possible collapse of the EU.

Since this chapter is reviewing forecasts on the Day After, it necessarily remains high on claims and opinion and rather short on facts.

MAINLY UK EXPECTATIONS

It may be best to start with a list of some reported impacts, always remembering that there was disagreement about whether they would all occur:

The reduced price of the pound means a more expensive foreign holiday.

Passports and driving licences will have to be changed in the future back to a UK format.

Visas may be needed to travel abroad.

Border checks entering Europe could be slower due to having to queue in the All Other Passports lanes.

Petrol and diesel will cost more at the pumps because of the devaluation of the pound against the dollar.

Savers' rates will reduce if base rates are cut and vice versa.

Mortgage costs could rise if base rates are raised and vice versa.

Shop prices will go up partly arising from increased transport costs due to fuel price rises and partly to reflect higher import costs with a lower pound.

Jobs will be less safe if Brexit triggers a recession.

It will become more difficult for EU citizens in the UK with new restrictions, permits and other costs being imposed.

<u>Author's note</u>: This is a particularly controversial claim as is the next one.

Access to the NHS and ability to get a job may be affected in due course for EU citizens in the UK.

Future immigration from the EU to the UK would be based on an Australian type of points system, as is already in place for non-EU migrants.

Britons living in the EU may have acquired rights including for residency and property but possibly excluding certain benefits in the future.

There is some question about healthcare rights for British citizens in the EU if the reciprocal arrangements come to an end due to Brexit.

It could be more expensive and difficult to move to the EU in terms of residency requirements, work permits and higher property taxes.

According to a TNS poll on 24 June, 50% of voters expect a new Tory leader to hold a general election.

Ian Duncan Smith, former Tory leader, felt that it would be best to start negotiations without delay for what was often referred to as a divorce from the EU. However, the PM, who was expecting to be in office until October, preferred the new PM to decide the timing of the Article 50 trigger notice. MEP Daniel Hannan suggested that although divergence begins now, nothing will actually change for two to three years. He wanted to carry Remainers with the Government during a steady phased process involving no sudden changes. Indeed, he stressed that it had never been said that the door would be shut to all immigrants, nor that there would be any impact on existing EU ones.

Although the dream ticket was Johnson (PM) and Gove (Chancellor), Cameron loyalists were rallying to Theresa May as the best choice for the next PM. Nicknamed Karla after John Le Carré's inscrutable Russian spymaster, she had supported Remain albeit with a low campaign profile.

The leaving process under Article 50 of the Lisbon Treaty has been in force since 2009 but there is no strict timetable. After the Article 50 Notification, the clock will run for two years whilst exit negotiations take place between the UK and the EU, probably as a whole. Unless an extension of time is agreed, the UK will leave the EU on the expiry of the two years, whether or not exit terms have been settled.

It amounts to a basic divorce only and does not include trade deals which have been known to take up to 20 years. Nor must it include terms about freedom of movement. There is another leaving method that was discussed: the repeal of the original 1973 enabling legislation followed by the retention or abolition of all subsequent EEC/EU legislation by ministerial decisions. However, few seemed to think that was viable or likely, bearing in mind that the UK remained bound by the Lisbon Treaty and its Article 50.

Approximate quotes are again taken from 24 June 2016.

"President Obama appears to have reneged on his threats to British voters ahead of the Referendum (back of the queue for a trade deal), now saying that US and UK are indispensable partners."

"The recovery of the markets proves that the economic warnings about Brexit from Cameron and Osborne were unfounded."

"Brexit could trigger a faster rise in state pension age."

"If we are out of the Single Market, air fares in Europe could rise by up to 30%."

"The Referendum demonstrates that the UK is a mature democracy and we must now go on to a healing process."

"With Scotland expected to leave after its own referendum, we could go from being a major player to being a little runt state."

"There will be little change in the near future because passports, pensions and mortgages will all be the same though petrol may go up a bit."

"Britain is likely to see a surge in immigration from other EU countries as Europeans look to get into the country before tighter controls are imposed."

"We can look forward to faster rates of economic growth as we embrace the world economy."

"The poorest voted for Brexit, now they will bear the brunt of the cost."

"Leaving the EU must give us more control including over terrorism."

"The long term is gloomy as farmers and food manufacturers lose their EU subsidies."

"We should look ahead to opportunities to trade more freely with the rest of the world."

"A lot of young people voted on Facebook but failed to vote in practice."

"Article 50 is an EU process that should be ignored as it is not necessary and would cause delay. The Civil Service should now be doing the groundwork for swiftly leaving the EU in our own way."

Quite a wide variety of issues were raised. There were negative predictions about the housing market with agents reporting sales falling through and buyers worrying about increases in mortgage rates leading to falling prices. The BBC reported on 24 June that Morgan Stanley were relocating 2,000 jobs from London to Frankfurt and Dublin but on the same day, the bank said that the report was untrue.

The London Mayor announced that every European resident in London was very welcome. However, one Eastern European, on being asked by a reporter if she was worried, replied "No, but I might go home." Heathrow expansion was now claimed to be essential to make the UK a super outward-looking power. It would bring £18 billion of private investment together with jobs, growth and stability. Some said that a general election may be called within the next six months.

And what of the future bearing in mind the existing so-called dysfunctional, unreformed and aloof EU? No wonder the Leave Side slogan, to take back control, was effective when the austerity, or they might say the cruelty, imposed by the EU on southern Europe was considered, e.g. extremely high unemployment in Greece. The method of doing this has been by use of the powers of the Troika comprising the European Central Bank (ECB), the European Commission (EC) and the International Monetary Fund (IMF) acting together. The Troika only made available bailout money on severe budgetary conditions which resulted in a Greek depression.

Why then should British workers worry about loss of EU protection of their workers' rights when so many EU citizens have lost their jobs because of the political wish to keep the euro? At least the pound can now definitely be retained without risk of a damaging EU policy change requiring the UK to join the Eurozone at a future date. It seemed that the majority of voters were pleased to imagine freedom from an EU-dominated future, one which they thought could easily have proved a bigger leap in the dark than a Brexit future.

"Within two or three years, the EU will be unrecognisable and the SNP boil will have been lanced."

"Scotland and England have never felt politically further apart."

"The England Nigel Farage represents is not the UK I want to be part of."

"Remain never made a case for Europe, only for not leaving it to avoid terrible things."

"I went to sleep on Thursday night in Great Britain and woke up on Friday morning in Little England."

J. P. Morgan Chase said that Brexit could mean UK staff changes over time.

A voter in Manchester remarked that what was <u>not</u> needed was the media using words like catastrophe and disaster. The Vote has been held and we just need to get on with it. One opinion of the Welsh preference for Brexit was that the economic benefit of EU money for Wales was outweighed by a wish for the return of sovereignty.

A Leaver in Manchester said he had voted against the Establishment and in favour of democracy; it really was one person one vote and the Remainers should accept the outcome. Had the Remainers won, he would have accepted it. The vitriol of the campaign should now be put behind us. Another said that he thought there would be a temporary recession but that was worth it to get our democracy back.

A Remainer in Manchester, which as a whole Voted Remain, commented that she did not trust politicians, felt that Brexit was inward-looking, was worried about the political climate and attitudes, considered there were many unknowns and was dismayed by the Leavers' back-tracking on allocating Brexit savings to the NHS. Another thought that the weakest and poorest would now be hit the most in a country that would have been stronger within the EU.

"There must be a Conservative leadership contest now and Boris Johnson is in pole position to become the Prime Minister. Many Tories see this as a near-certainty despite there being a significant following for Home Secretary, Theresa May."

"There is a real chance of another General Election by autumn."

A view, from Debenhams the department store, stressed the sheer division in society with the young wishing to Remain. There were also specific needs for calm, for more certainty, for a new PM, for a redefining of relationships and for a reduction in spending by shoppers.

A view, from Legal and General, was that the UK now had a simple choice between taking a positive route or a negative one. If the former, Brexit would be successful due to the opportunities; if the latter, there would be failure.

"It is now essential to revert to the traditional British blue passport in order to identify the nationality of all wanting to cross our borders."

"In the difficult days which lie ahead, it will be essential to protect UK working conditions which will be at risk from a Conservative Government."

"A large body of EU inspired legislation will have to be dealt with in the two year period allowed for implementing Brexit. It will be difficult."

Both Labour and UKIP considered that they should be involved in the Brexit negotiations. On the Conservative side, Johnson and Gove were preparing a "dream team" to take over leadership of the Party.

Brexit will cause certain practical consequences about how things are run: after the Article 50 notice to leave and the two year negotiation period have expired, the UK will be released from all EU treaty obligations; until then, everything will carry on without change including free movement, free trade and MEPs; the negotiated terms of exit must be approved by all 27 states, any one of which could veto them; the Cameron Deal, on which he fought the Referendum, is now null and void.

"The next government will be the most pro-globalisation in recent history."

"Mrs. Merkel thinks there are no simple or fast conclusions to draw from Brexit. She is wrong. There is a simple conclusion for the EU. The choice is to reform or die."

"The Referendum has demonstrated the political cartel that exists in the UK. People should be allowed to choose the policies they prefer and not be limited to those put forward by the Westminster Elite. From now on, any party, that reflects public opinion in this way, will prosper."

"The Chancellor of the Exchequer, George Osborne, should continue to hold his office for the next few weeks to ensure some continuity."

"What matters now is to protect the poor in society."

"The banks can be expected to move some jobs from London to Europe."

"A recession is now inevitable because foreign investors will refuse to finance Britain's yawning current account deficit."

"The big question is what happens on the ground and whether the mooted recession really arrives."

"Britain must seize this chance to exploit its unique status as an English-speaking powerhouse midway between New York and Asia."

"I am a student and feel unwanted by the UK."

"Leave won because anger trumped fear."

"It is important now to ensure that the politicians don't negotiate us back into the EU."

"Here is a country so imbalanced, it has effectively fallen over."

"Opinion polling is a dismal science which should be set aside. It is not about percentages and leading questions — it is time people went into the country and simply listened."

"This is not about sovereignty but immigration. Brexit has set expectations which must not now be fudged by the politicians. As understood by millions, this is a mandate to reduce immigration dramatically. There is nothing abstract here. We need clear net migration targets, clear means of achieving them and clear dates those targets will be hit."

"In Wales, it will not only be very important to reassess the Barnett Formula and the areas benefitting presently from EU money (where the Leave Vote was unexpectedly strong), but also the Devolved Assembly will need to be on a different footing. There needs to be a promise that Wales will not lose money."

"No-one ever presented the pros and cons of membership fairly and comprehensively. All we heard was propaganda."

"If there's one good thing about Brexit, it is that the Hinckley Point C nuclear disaster will never get built."

"We need a trade agreement as soon as possible with a major nation thus boosting confidence that the UK will thrive outside the EU, even if it is post-dated to the leaving date. Certainly, the vast majority of economists opposing Brexit will be proved completely wrong within the next five years."

"The country can unite after this result as has happened before with General Elections. It would help however to bring in to Government both the Remainers and industrialists, i.e. to make Brexit work."

"So, Scotland might leave the UK. What about a universal declaration of independence from London?"

"Leavers kept telling me they didn't expect it to happen. A lot of people are worrying about it just a bit."

"If there is one lesson that should be drawn from all this, it is that the usual rituals of the EU simply won't do."

"The shock waves are hitting an EU which is already weak and having trouble with the migration crisis and euro crisis. Euroscepticism is on the rise with calls for referendums in France, Italy and The Netherlands. Is there a future for EU?"

"It is likely that there will be a majority wanting to leave the EU in other countries, e.g. The Netherlands for a Nexit, Denmark for a Dexit and the same even in Austria, Sweden and Italy. We could now be seeing the beginning of the death of the EU, such that history will judge Brexit as the first step on the road to independent sovereign states. We now need a Brexit Government."

Sinn Fein claimed that the Vote intensified the case for Northern Ireland (NI) to leave the UK and become part of Ireland. The English votes may have dragged NI out of Europe but 56% Voted Remain thus justifying a border poll. Sinn Fein also contended that such a NI referendum would not be destabilising and could be conducted in a civilised way. Already on 24 June, many residents in NI were queueing for Irish passports as permitted under the Good Friday Agreement, presumably in order to have the greater flexibility arising from dual citizenship, or simply to retain EU citizenship.

"Will there need to be an international border established between Ireland and Northern Ireland including customs checks? Will there be a poll on a united Ireland?"

Donald Trump, U.S. Republican candidate for President, said that he had forecast the Leave result, thought it was a great thing and felt the British people had taken back their country.

SCOTTISH QUESTION

"There could be a second referendum for Scottish Independence because 62% in Scotland Voted Remain".

Clearly, the claim is that Brexit is democratically unacceptable to Scotland which voted the other way. Hence the idea of a second referendum is on the table.

Many Scots voted to stay in the UK in the 2014 Scottish Independence Referendum because they were told that independence would mean expulsion from the EU. They now feel betrayed because they will be leaving anyway due to the 2016 UK Referendum. As a matter of law, it may be a material change in circumstances justifying a second independence vote.

But is Scotland outside the UK and inside the EU a practicality? Since any second referendum to enable such an outcome would be the last, it is not likely to be called by the SNP if there is any real chance of losing it. Moreover, EU consent to admit Scotland would probably be a pre-condition for any second referendum and it might well not be granted. In addition, Westminster probably has first to agree to a fresh referendum.

The two problems last time were oil and currency, both unresolved and both made more difficult by Brexit.

Firstly, the significance of oil. The current oil price crash is likely to be long-term due to the depressing effect on the price of crude oil caused by the rise of fracking. Hence, this oil revenue would be unable to make up for the loss of the big fiscal subsidy of some £15 billion p.a. now given in effect by England to Scotland. Under the Barnett Formula, Scotland receives much more public money than England per head and can thus, unlike England, afford free prescriptions, University tuition fees and care for the elderly. It is an indefensible arrangement that has been resented by the English for a long time. In addition to finding this sum, through tax rises or spending cuts, the EU would be likely to expect a substantial Scottish contribution.

Secondly, the significance of the euro. Is it credible that the Scots would vote to leave the UK and agree to change to the euro? Put another way, can Scotland address Brexit by trying to leave the UK? There again, can the 62% for Remain be expected to translate to a similar figure for independence from the UK and would the serious problems of the euro be seen by the Scots as acceptable? These are the loss of economic sovereignty due to having no flexible exchange rate, an EU fixed interest rate, and no Scottish control over spending and taxation if an IMF bailout becomes necessary.

It may indeed suit the SNP best to get a Westminster refusal to hold a referendum.

EU EXPECTATIONS

It appears that the EU's worries about its very future existence, post-Brexit, were greater than those arising from a changed relationship with the UK. Since these worries are so important and took a few days to unfold, I am making an exception to the Day After limit for the book in order to give some brief details up to approx. 29 June.

At emergency talks in Brussels in the morning of Friday 24 June, there was a sense of shock, disbelief and sadness leading to worries over the risk of the EU breaking up. On the Monday, there were crisis talks in Berlin between Merkel and Tusk followed by more discussion between Merkel, Hollande and Renzi, the Italian PM.

The French right wing party, National Front issued a poster showing two fists rising from the water of the EU. The (presumably EU) shackles binding the wrists were broken, the word BREXIT was given a large green tick and the slogan was "ET MAINTENANT LA FRANCE". The message that France could, should and would follow the British lead and leave the EU was very clear.

Farage spoke controversially and in detail to the EU Parliament on Tuesday 28 June with a succinct summary of the UKIP view of Brexit. He was heard despite some barracking. Perhaps his most useful suggestion was for pragmatism on all sides and for a tariff free deal to be struck in the future to the benefit of both the EU and the UK. Despite the calls for quiet from the meeting's Chairman Schulz and for the members not to behave like UKIP, Farage was still not heard in silence; there was no denying the anger at his key part in Brexit. He sat down to boos and a minority of clapping.

Later on the same day, Cameron addressed the European Council in his usual statesmanlike manner in order to explain Brexit. Despite being shaken, EU leaders were determined to preserve the union of the remaining 27 nations. In an early recognition of the forthcoming UK departure, the EU summit continued the next day 29 June but without the presence of the PM. It was in order for the heads of state or government to consider the way ahead in terms of Article 50 and to reflect on the future of the EU.

Whilst France and Germany were willing to discuss trade at the same time as the Exit, the EU said that trade talks could not start until the Exit talks had finished.

There were fears in Paris, where President Hollande was chairing his cabinet, that instead of more integration, they were now facing disintegration. A very quick separation was thought essential so that France could avoid any contagion, i.e. pressure for a French referendum. The Front described Brexit as a historic moment, a new reality for all and proof that it is possible to leave the EU.

Whilst regretting Brexit, Hollande pointed out that the EU now had both to reaffirm its values of peace, freedom and tolerance and to make changes: "To move forward, Europe cannot act as before." This would mean no more lofty speeches, big visions, conventions and treaties. Prime Minister M. Valls referred to the breakup, pure and simple, of the Union.

Italian PM Renzi said Europe must be made "more human and more just." The Pope called for guarantees for the good of both the UK and the EU. Spain claimed Brexit meant the sovereignty of Gibraltar should be shared. The IMF welcomed the interventions of the Bank of England and the European Central Bank to aid stability and said the situation would continue to be monitored.

Poland's ambassador was most unhappy at Brexit and concerned for the acquired rights of its nationals in the UK. However, he remarked that Poland and Britain shared the same philosophy and goodwill would continue because Britain would still be in Europe, the G7, the G20 and NATO. Warsaw reacted with shock and concern for the one million Poles now in the UK and the useful $1 billion p.a. they sent back to Poland. There were questions about changes to travel and work permits.

There was talk in Berlin of the possibility of the EU breaking up and that things would not be made easy for the UK. Leaving negotiations would be tough. However, there were also German demands for no future trade barriers with the UK. Another German comment was that Brexit meant that the EU now appears to be "a bloc that cannot be relied upon". In a signal for the need to compromise, Angela Merkel referred to Europe as varied including in its expectations of the EU. A German strategy paper recommended that the UK be made an Associated Partner Country of the EU whilst citing concerns that others could follow Brexit, i.e. France, Austria, Finland, The Netherlands and Hungary.

Despite the misgivings of the Mayor of Calais, the French government announced that the existing Le Touquet agreement, between UK and France for the city's migrant camp, would continue. This meant that there was no longer a risk, as claimed by Remainers before the Referendum, of shifting the border control point from France to SE England with all the chaos that would ensue. The camp, known as the Jungle, is a rather lawless tented complex providing poor living conditions for thousands of would-be migrants, many of whom are illegals from outside the EU.

Some key members of the EU wanted Brexit negotiations to begin at once. However, when the PM talked of that being for the next PM to decide in October, German Chancellor Merkel was sympathetic to that timescale.

"The British voting is like their cooking: absolutely terrible." French comment

"The EU has to change or it will die."

"The British people have given to the Europeans and also to the world a dazzling lesson in democracy."

"As a Pole, I now feel uncomfortable."

"Coming from Germany, we feel let down. Being rejected doesn't feel so nice."

"Although there is no wish in Europe 'to punish the UK,' the 'domino effect' must be considered. This means that a good exit deal cannot be agreed for UK because that would encourage other states to leave."

"To be honest I'm going back to Germany in four weeks. I expected more support from you guys."

"They'll want to keep me because I'm a doctor but why should I stay when I have no rights?"

Enough has been said to show that those inside the EU know that they may well have to fight a "contagion of referendums pulling apart the bloc."

One view inside the EU is that Brexit is a wake-up call from the many citizens who feel disenfranchised. Under this view, Brexit is said to be good for Europe because it gives the message that people want less, not more integration, a message that has always emerged whenever EU citizens have had a chance to give an opinion. Indeed, it is only the European Parliament and the EU elite who press for more integration. If anything, the failure of the EU means that Schulz, President of the European Parliament, and Juncker, President of the European Commission, should step down. Of the 51 countries in Europe, only 28 are in the EU; those outside, including Norway and Switzerland, can and do survive perfectly well.

Considerable anger with the PM was expressed in some quarters of the EU. He was accused of being irresponsible, not a good leader, someone who quit leaving a mess behind and shamefully sought early retirement rather than immediately serving notice under Article 50. Brexit was claimed in these quarters to be a huge mistake because no country is big enough on its own to take major decisions: sovereignty has to be pooled.

Comments from Mr. Schulz were not very positive: the UK is on a dangerous path; a whole continent should not be taken hostage because of an internal fight in the Tory Party; Britons must face consequences in order to avoid a chain reaction of referendums; Britain is barred from arranging trade deals until the end of the two year period triggered by Article 50. Whilst the European Parliament is very sad, he recognised the sovereign will of the UK voters. It will now be necessary for the EU to discuss improvements and how to protect the EU at a meeting of the four Presidents.

President of the European Council, Donald Tusk, had wanted a different outcome but stressed that the EU was no fair-weather project. He said that the 27 states are determined to carry on whilst EU law will apply to the UK until withdrawal has taken place.

The right wing party leaders in Europe were very keen to capitalise on the Brexit outcome. Speaking from France, Holland, Denmark, Italy and Sweden, they referred to: a Victory for Liberty; Long Live the Courage of Free Citizens; it is our turn next; the EU underestimated Euroscepticism; we need to renegotiate and follow with a referendum as was done by the UK, and so forth. Poll after poll shows from a third to a half of the population in many European countries share a "British" mistrust of the EU. One comment from Germany was that Merkel expelled Britain from the EU with her open borders. This referred to Mrs. Merkel's much-criticised open invitation for migrants to settle in Germany, an invitation which seemed to create an enormous increase in migration from outside the EU to both Germany and the UK.

REACTIONS OF KEY POLITICIANS

The following descriptions do not repeat the exact phraseology of these post-Referendum speakers. However, my intention is to convey some of the main sense or meaning of their speeches on the day after the Vote.

Boris Johnson (Conservative key member of Vote Leave)

I pay tribute to David Cameron's work and was sad to see him step down. The PM, who was indeed brave to give the Referendum to the country, was leaving in his wake the most dynamic economy in Europe. I also thank the people for answering this tough question.

Although some say it was wrong to ask the Leave question, I suggest instead that it was right and inevitable, concerning as it did the restoration of democratic control over key decisions; the EU is opaque, remote and unaccountable. There is no current need for haste because nothing will change in the short term. Nor will the UK be less united, less European or more isolationist. The opposite is true as we will still be part of Europe.

Great Britain can be a great European power without any need for a federal government system like the EU. We shall be open and friendly with lots of travel possible on the continent. The young especially need to realise that democratic control will mean more security and prosperity. Their future will be better under such control. It is a glorious opportunity as we shall find our own voice for decisions on laws, taxes and borders. Our borders will be controlled through a fair and non-discriminatory system which will take the wind out of the sails of those extremists who would play politics with immigration.

As the world's fifth biggest economy, we shall be powerful, liberal and humane. After all, it was this country which gave parliamentary democracy to Europe.

Michael Gove (Conservative key member of Vote Leave)

I also pay tribute to the outgoing PM and would emphasise that the Government has been given a very clear instruction by the people. This is only the start of the process and existing trade will continue for now in the same way as before.

Since it will be necessary to secure the best terms for Britain's exit from the EU, we should use wisdom from outside politics. We have always been an open country, believing in free trade and a humane immigration policy. As a self-governing democracy we shall be well-placed to continue to resist oppression.

I should like to reassure the young. By taking a sober and calming approach, I believe that there will be better relations with Europe when the country becomes self-reliant and not in any way embittered.

Gisela Stuart (Labour key member of Vote Leave)

This has been a huge democratic exercise and an extraordinary democratic opportunity. In Vote Leave, we acted for the whole country, not for any sectional interest. We have also been looking to what is in the best interests of Europe and wish to continue as good neighbours to our friends on the continent.

Nigel Farage (Leader of UK Independence Party)

The Sun has risen on an Independent UK; this is a victory for ordinary decent people; the Old Labour voters have turned out for Leave in the West Midlands and the North; people have shown courage to do the right thing, proving the disconnect between Westminster and real communities; it is a vote against mass immigration with its consequences of lower wages, inability to get kids into local schools and trouble with getting an appointment to see a GP.

I give the credit for the result to Labour voters. I am delighted with the outcome of my 25 year campaign to Leave the EU and here is a suggestion:

"23 June should be a national Bank Holiday called Independence Day"

Jean-Claude Juncker (President of the European Commission)

I regret this decision by the UK but respect it at the same time. There should be no delay in its implementation as this will just create uncertainty. Therefore, the UK should act as quickly as possible however painful that process may be. But Britain will be treated like a deserter. The February 2016 settlement with Cameron has ceased to have any effect.

Although I hold out no prospect of re-negotiation, I hope that the UK will be a close EU partner in the future. A balanced agreement will be needed where France and Germany will take a clear position. The BBC ask whether this is the beginning of the end for the EU – my answer is "No". The core values of the EU will be upheld including peace, security, prosperity and the environment.

Nicola Sturgeon (First Minister of Scotland)

In Scotland, we value the contribution of immigrants and Voted Remain after a positive campaign. But Westminster must search its soul in order to respond to the democratic position of Scotland. That position is unacceptable because in the recent Scottish Independence Referendum, many Scots voted to stay in the UK in order to keep within the EU. Had they voted for independence, we were told that EU membership would have been lost.

Not only shall I do all I can to keep Scotland in the EU and Single Market, I shall be exploring a second independence referendum for Scotland as justified by the significant change caused by the Leave Vote. A Yes vote would mean a review of the Scottish border with England. After the fear and hate of the campaign, I will act to unite Scotland which should be a modern, outward-looking and proud nation. If the Scottish Parliament wants another independence referendum, that may not need the approval of Westminster. It is my responsibility to act in the best interests of Scotland.

Angela Merkel

I have great regret at the Referendum result but we must now keep calm and analyse the decisions needed. Undue haste could increase rifts in the EU. Let's not beat around the bush. Today marks a turning point for Europe and the project of European unity. There are varied expectations within the EU such that other countries, apart from UK, also have doubts. One question is how can we improve the lives of EU citizens?

The whole idea for the EU comes from a wish for peace after centuries of conflict and a world in turmoil. Even now, the effects of the wars in Europe are still felt. But the EU is strong enough to find the right answers. As for the Leave process, the rights and obligations of the leaving member will stay the same until that member is removed.

11   Reflection

"By three methods we may learn wisdom: first, by reflection, which is noblest;
second, by imitation, which is easiest;
and third by experience, which is the bitterest."

Confucius

Since the basis of the book is (with one small exception in the previous chapter) not to stray beyond 24 June 2016, it is inappropriate to try and summarise what has happened between that date and the time of publication. I wanted to avoid any sort of hindsight or backdated comparison of the merits of the Leave and Remain contentions. Certainly, any such summary would soon enough be out of date. Hence, since this short chapter is no more than a brief look back at the whole affair, I hope the reader will not feel short-changed by the lack of definite conclusions, lessons or projections. Opinions on those matters really are for the politicians, the journalists, the reader and history.

The Referendum of 23 June 2016 was a revealing democratic exercise that gave a real picture of the UK at that time. Despite the enormous level of publicity on TV, radio, in the newspapers and other publications, that picture was not particularly distorted by the media or special interest groups. Votes seem to have been cast depending on the location, age group and people's personal experiences of the EU.

125

It was obvious that generally the youngest were Remainers and the oldest Leavers. London, Scotland, Northern Ireland and Gibraltar had their reasons to Remain whilst most of the rest of the country favoured Leave. A key result was that apart from London and a few other islands of Remainers, England was solidly for Leave no doubt because those voters did not see the EU as an advantage to them or the country.

Paradoxically, the UK appeared to be both united and divided at one and the same time. Although there was often much more heat than light in the debates, there was also a great wish to try and do the Right Thing. Moreover, once the result was known, the great majority wanted to unite and get behind the Leave decision for the good of all. This positive outlook, reminiscent of the normal post-election discussion in America (between the new President and the unsuccessful candidate), must be a good sign for the future of the UK. That said however, some Remainers were voluble in wanting to overturn the result.

The Referendum had its strange and tragic aspects. The murder of Jo Cox MP shocked everyone and may have helped the Remainers. Some thought Leave had won because of Labour voters going against party policy whilst others thought the main reason was the popular Boris Johnson combined with the controversial Nigel Farage.

The biggest single issue was uncontrolled immigration. Yet little was made of the fact that there is more migration, which is already supposed to be controlled, from non-EU countries than from the EU itself. Nor of the massive illegal immigration which has not been tackled effectively by the Government. If the Government is not able to stem these two big flows which should be within its control, what hope is there for stemming EU migration post-Brexit?

It is also curious that the main political reason for joining the EEC in 1973, to be an influential bridge between America and Europe, was never mentioned.

The turnout was extremely good at 72% reflecting the high degree of interest in the outcome. Everyone saying anything of importance was held to account by the Press so that few stones were left unturned. For example, anyone wanting to find out about the claimed £350 million per week UK contribution to the EU could do so. Owing to the broad success of the public relations campaign for Remain, few were expecting Leave to win. As a result, the Leave victory created a quite a shock, followed by great surprise at the sheer democratic power of the Referendum, as displayed by its consequences on the Day After.

In the end, the significance of the Referendum outcome of Brexit will be judged by history. Was it a good democratic decision showing the collective wisdom of British voters?

Although the only way to answer that is by revealing one's own opinion on the merits of Brexit, there is another equally intriguing question: why did the Leavers win? My personal answer would be that rightly or wrongly, due to the force of history and the continuing sense of national identity, most voters wanted all policies to be decided in the UK in a democratic fashion. I think that this was a weighty argument which carried the day because unlike the various other contentions, this one could not be disputed.

This is why I chose a photograph of Big Ben (Elizabeth Tower) above some people at the Houses of Parliament for the front cover. Coincidentally, the Number 211 double decker bus in the picture is headed for the terminus of Waterloo.

INDEX

Article 50, Lisbon Treaty   82, 99, 107, 109, 112, 117, 120
Australian style points system   57, 62, 106

Balance and bias   3, 6
Bamford, Lord Anthony   10
Belgium   42, 49
Belloc, Hilaire   48
Benefits of EU   24-27, 29, 30, 34, 35, 107
Big Ben (Elizabeth Tower)   127
BMW   33
Breaking Point Claim   54, 59, 83, 103
Brexit consequences   12, 81, 85, 101, 112
British Constitution   39, 40
Bureaucracy   5, 15, 52, 57, 94

Cameron, David   4, 24, 26, 29, 65-67, 82, 90, 91, 93, 98, 117, 123
Campaign   3, 21, 55, 61, 92
Churchill, Winston   3, 6, 39, 41
Common Market   42, 49
Conservative Party   13, 15-17, 40, 44, 89, 111
Context of debate   36, 39
Contributions to EU   20, 43, 59, 127
Corbyn, Jeremy   21, 66-68, 75, 76, 100, 101
Corruption   14, 15, 58, 78
Cox, Jo   21-23, 126
Crux, The   3
Cummings, Dominic   63, 64

Day After 23 June 2016   81
de Gaulle, Charles   42
Democracy   3, 6, 12, 14, 19, 35, 39-41, 51, 59, 63, 67, 78, 87, 88, 91, 92, 98, 110, 121, 122
Devaluation   31, 87, 106
Duncan Smith, Ian   107
Dyson, James 10

Education   55, 56, 76, 77

Elliott, Matthew   63, 64
Emergency budget   32, 65, 93
English Channel   37, 39, 40
EU aeroplane crash cartoon   92
EU apple regulations   57, 58
EU costs   15, 59
EU election 2014   83
EU expectations   116
EU members   4
Euro   13-15, 24-26, 43, 44, 49, 50, 90, 116
European Arrest Warrant   28, 67
European Central Bank   43, 51, 109, 118
European Commission   43, 51, 109, 119, 123
European Constitution   90
Eurozone members   4
Exchange Rate Mechanism   43

Farage, Nigel   4, 10, 35, 54, 59, 62-64, 67, 82-84, 88, 92, 116, 117,
          122, 126
Fishing industry   51, 67
France   42, 49, 54, 90, 116-118, 123

General Elections   6, 9, 17, 43-45, 66, 69, 83, 86, 90, 101, 109
GPs, access to   36, 54, 122
Germany   15, 42, 49, 117, 119, 120, 123
Gibraltar   73, 74, 117, 126
Gove, Michael   85, 92, 107, 111
Government pamphlet   4, 20, 67
Greece   15, 26, 49, 50, 109

Hannan, Daniel   107
Heath, Edward   42
History, force of   5, 15, 37, 45, 127
Hollande, Francois   116, 117
Hospitals   14, 53, 59, 64
Housing   13, 14, 56, 66, 73, 74, 77, 88, 109
Human rights   13, 16

Ice age   37

Immigration   5, 12, 13, 14, 17, 21, 27, etc.
In Campaign Ltd., The   10, 66
International Monetary Fund   29, 43, 98, 109, 116, 117,
Italy   42, 49, 97, 114, 120

Jingoism   38, 39
Jobs and exports   29, 31, 67
Johnson, Boris   21, 64, 66, 88, 92, 99, 107, 111, 121, 126
Juncker, Jean-Claude   119, 123

Labour Party   4, 15, 21, 40, 42-45, 66-68, 75, 76, 83, 89, 100-102,
                111, 122
Labour, campaign lacklustre   21, 100
Labour, motion of no confidence   100
Leadsom, Andrea   10, 11
Leave.EU   11, 62, 63, 84
Leavers, both sombre and jubilant   3, 83, 92
Leavers, top ten areas   71, 73, 74, 77
Liberal Democrat Party   4, 11, 21, 63, 90
Lisbon Treaty (see also Article 50 above)   82, 90, 107, 108
Little Englanders   29, 35, 52
Local quotes on 24 June 2016   86
London   20, 30, 63, 69, 72-74, 97, 100, 109, 126
Looking Ahead   105
Looking Back   87
Lost Democracy   98
Low Wages   14, 53
Luxembourg   42, 49

Macmillan, Harold   42
Main Players   9, 36
Major, John   43
Martin, Tim (Wetherspoons)   10
Merkel, Angela   112, 116, 118, 120, 124
Metropolitan Elite   20, 71, 74

NHS claim by Leavers   5, 59, 64, 127
Netherlands, The   42, 49, 114, 118
Norman Conquest, 1066   38, 39

Northern Ireland   29, 69, 73, 105, 114, 126

Obama Barack   22, 30, 65
Osborne, George   32, 65, 89, 104

Patriotism   37-39, 44
Pensions   32, 33, 93, 108
Perceived needs   13
Poland   44, 55, 118
Political integration   27, 28
Polls   45, 66, 74, 87, 89
Pound   26, 31, 34, 43, 85, 89, 101, 110
Project Fear   30, 32, 35, 48, 64-66, 77, 87-88

Racists   35, 54, 90, 98, 105
Red tape   25, 28, 50, 51
Referendum 1975   42, 44, 49, 91
Referendums, contagion of   117, 119
Reflection   125
Remain website   67
Remainers, anger of some   3, 88, 99
Remainers, top ten areas   72
Renegotiation by PM   24, 25, 65, 91
Romans   37
Rudd, Amber   10, 11

Safer in EU   28, 82
Schengen Agreement   25, 26, 34
Schulz, Martin   117, 119, 120
Scotland   69, 73, 85, 105, 115, 123
Scottish Referendum 2014   11, 66, 85, 115, 123
Separation of powers   40
Single Market   20, 26, 28, 29, 31-34, 52, 78, 87, 101, 103, 123
Slums for immigrants   56
Social Democrats   43
Sovereignty   14, 19, 24, 29, 34-36, 43, 44, 49, 63, 66, 87, 90, 98, 110, 116, 117, 120
Spain   74, 97, 117
Stiglitz, Joseph   43

Stock market   31, 85-87, 97, 101
Strasbourg Parliament   14, 15
Stronger in Europe   4, 10, 66, 67, 82, 111
Stuart, Gisela   10, 11, 92, 122
Sturgeon, Nicola   10, 11, 123

Take Back Control   5, 52, 54, 63, 93, 109
Thatcher, Margaret   43, 91, 98
Trade deals with Japan and USA   30
Travel within EU   29, 30, 36, 82, 118, 121
Treaty of Rome 1957   24, 42, 44
Troika   43, 109
Trump, Donald   114
Turkey   39, 52, 64
Tusk, Donald   116, 120

Uncertainty Issue   20, 48, 62
UKIP   4, 5, 11, 41, 54, 62, 64, 73, 78, 83, 90, 92, 97, 111, 116, 117
Underdog theory   62, 63, 65

Victory for the Common Man   97
Vote, The 23 June 2016   69
Vote by age   75
Vote by party   75
Vote by time of decision   76
Vote Leave Case   47
Vote Leave Ltd.   11
Vote Remain Case   19
Vote, timetable after vote   84

Wales   73, 97, 110, 113
Welfare restrictions   4, 27, 67
Wilson, Harold   42, 44, 91
Workers' rights   27, 103, 110
World war prevention   23, 24, 40, 41, 102